T0327904

SEA MAGICK

Connect With the Ocean Through Folklore
and Magickal Traditions

Rieka Moonsong

ROCK
POINT

First published in 2024 by Rock Point, an imprint of The Quarto Group,
142 West 36th Street, 4th Floor, New York, NY 10018, USA • (212) 779-4972 www.Quarto.com

Rock Point titles are also available at discount for retail, wholesale, promotional, and bulk purchase. For details, contact the Special Sales Manager by email at specialsales@quarto.com or by mail at The Quarto Group, Attn: Special Sales Manager, 100 Cummings Center Suite 265D, Beverly, MA 01915 USA.

10 9 8 7 6 5 4 3 2 1

ISBN: 978-1-57715-470-9

Digital edition published in 2024
eISBN: 978-0-76039-225-6

Library of Congress Cataloging-in-Publication Data

Names: Moonsong, Rieka, author.
Title: Sea magick : connect with the ocean through
    folklore and magickal traditions / Rieka Moonsong.
Description: New York, NY : Rock Point, 2024. | Includes bibliographical
    references and index. | Summary: "Sea Magick explores the magickal
    qualities of the largest bodies of water from the element of water, sea
    deities, mythical creatures, sea animals and plants, and more"--
    Provided by publisher.
Identifiers: LCCN 2024009901 (print) | LCCN 2024009902 (ebook) | ISBN
    9781577154709 (hardcover) | ISBN 9780760392256 (ebook)
Subjects: LCSH: Ocean--Folklore. | Ocean--Mythology. | Sea monsters.
Classification: LCC GR910 .M645 2024 (print) | LCC GR910 (ebook) | DDC
    398/.322--dc23/eng/20240402
LC record available at https://lccn.loc.gov/2024009901
LC ebook record available at https://lccn.loc.gov/2024009902

Group Publisher: Rage Kindelsperger
Editorial Director: Erin Canning
Creative Director: Laura Drew
Managing Editor: Cara Donaldson
Editor: Katelynn Abraham
Cover Design: Marisa Kwek
Interior Design: Wendy Lai
Cover Illustration: Maggie Vandewalle

Printed in China

DEDICATION

This book, as always, is dedicated to my children, Hailey and Jake. You will always be the greatest thing I have ever created. I am so proud of you both and love you so very much. This book is also dedicated to our Ocean Mother. May she flourish in health and may her power, wisdom, and calming energy continue to flow to those willing to be open to her.

CONTENTS

PROLOGUE

She calls to you. She is both a lullaby and a raging torrent in the same breath. Your feet meet the sand, still warm from the heat of the Sun that is now dipping below the horizon, painting the sky with pink, orange, and gold, his reflection setting the waters ablaze.

Your bare feet delight in the sugary texture as they make their way across the stretch of sand. The gulls sound overhead, searching for one last snack to end the day. The tangy smell of the salty air welcomes you as the breeze whips around, playing with your hair.

The waves roll in, steady and sure, beating in rhythm with your heart. As you draw near the water's edge, you feel the pull, the longing that never quite goes away. The waves gently kiss your feet, lapping around your ankles and strengthening the pull you feel. With your feet upon the shore and arms raised to the sky, you answer her, "Ocean Mother, I am here."

Stripping down to venture out, your soul finally feels at peace. With one deep breath, you dive beneath the waves and hear, "Welcome home, my child."

INTRODUCTION

Hello and merry meet. I am so happy and extremely honored that this book has made its way to you. If it has, you may be a beginner or a practitioner who has previously worked with ocean energy. Or maybe you are simply looking to dive deeper (pun intended). For whatever reason you have opened this book, there is something to be found here within its pages that is just for you.

The oceans and seas are powerful forces to have with you in your magickal practice. Within these pages, you'll learn how to work with the water element to ease yourself into the great power of the ocean. There are many influential traits that make up the ocean, such as the tides, waves, composition, and darkness, that you can seek guidance from in your magickal practice. You will learn about the various deities tied to the sea as well as how to work with them.

With thrilling stories of the deep, including Atlantis, the Bermuda Triangle, and the Sargasso Sea, you will find that sea magick has a deep history full of wonder. Along the way, you may discover that you are one of the souls of Atlantis or had a previous life as one of the merfolk. Maybe you lived a life as a sailor on the high seas but met a tragic end when a raging storm took your ship. Along this journey, you will not only find information on how to seek this knowledge but also learn how to heal from aspects of it that may be troubling you today.

For those witches who already practice with plants and animals, this book will expand your reach to those beneath the sea, including creatures some consider to be found only in myths and legends. Learn what they can bring to your magickal workings and how to call upon them. Even through a collection of seashells, the vastness with which the oceans hold will soon be revealed to you.

From the beach to the inky black depths, from the waves to sea caves and tide pools. The energy of the oceans and seas is as wonderful and vast as she is, and the knowledge within these places is almost endless. Learn spells and rituals to work with all aspects of the oceans and seas and further incorporate her power into your workings.

Form a bond with the sea, and the path to becoming a sea witch may present itself to you. As a water sign (Scorpio) myself, with a deep love for the ocean and all its mystery and magick, I take working with her and her energies very seriously, but that doesn't mean we won't have any fun! So, don your metaphysical goggles and snorkels, and let's explore the might of sea magick!

WHAT IS SEA MAGICK?

Millions of years ago, life began to stir within the sea, evolving and growing. While our lives eventually pulled us away from our Ocean Mother, for some, the call to come back is not something that can be ignored.

Sea magick is the call that one feels deep in their soul to work with the power of the water element in a completely different way. It's the siren's song that you must answer when you hear it, for it will lead you to a place that feels like home. Sea magick is attuning yourself to the tides, the ebb and flow, and the rhythm of the waves. It becomes a knowing that you are made of the sea, for the same salt runs through your veins.

For a little geography, the oceans and seas cover 70 percent of our planet. Of all the water found on Earth, 96.5 percent is within the oceans and seas, with 1 percent in freshwater lakes and rivers. Our total water surface is 71 percent. With a total surface area of 197 million square miles (510 million square km), compared to the 58 million square miles (150 million square km) of our land masses, how can one not feel drawn to work with water in some capacity?[1] Within these pages, we'll dive in much deeper and learn all about the element and the vastness of its power that spans this world.

◦◇ WORKING WITH THE WATER ELEMENT ◇◦

Most witches probably incorporate the water element in their practice to some degree, with some more comfortable working with it than others. Traditionally, there are four core elements that make up the world: air, water, earth, and fire. We witches have an added fifth element: spirit. Some might feel an affinity for one element over the others or have an easier time connecting with it and its magick. Whichever element you are most connected to, know that each is essential to life on the surface and in the metaphysical realm.

We witches love to make our Moon water. We also tend to discuss our zodiac signs, where three of the twelve—Pisces, Cancer, and Scorpio—are water signs. Yet, this is just the surface of water's power.

Water is a powerful force of nature. As you learn to work with water, you will learn all of her personality. She will tell you her secrets and show you where her power lies and how to use it. Much like the element of fire, water should be respected and never taken for granted. One of the many benefits of working with water is how much she can teach you about yourself, life, and the world around you.

One of the many aspects that water rules over, in a metaphysical sense, is emotions. You will learn how to balance emotions by working closely with her. Do you need to calm the raging storm, or is it time to open the floodgates a little wider because you have been holding back too much? Water signs of the zodiac know what a challenge this can be. For those that are not water signs, use this element instead to balance other areas in your chart.

Learn the significance of the ebb and flow and how it can be applied to our life. We see how things quickly become icky if they are left stagnant. We must adapt and flow to develop what we seek. And we can do all this without losing our essential nature. Change is necessary, and we must remain patient, as it can often take time to make it happen.

WATER AND THE DIVINE FEMININE

You may have noticed that I have been using the pronoun, she, when referring to water. This element is considered to be feminine in nature. Earth is also a feminine element, while air and fire are both masculine. This has nothing to do with actual gender but the overall characteristic of the metaphysical and energetic properties.

The overall energy of water resonates with that of the Moon and its lunar cycles and phases. It is a being that holds powerful Divine Feminine energy—the power of the goddesses, creation, and the cycle of life, death, and rebirth. Further, the thirteen moons in a calendar year are each twenty-eight days long, which is roughly the length of a menstruation cycle. While some cultures also have masculine lunar deities, the majority of those associated with the Moon are feminine. Well-known lunar goddesses are Luna, Selene, Diana, Artemis, and Hekate. Working with the element of water may help you understand Moon energies on a different level as well as that of the Divine Feminine. It can also help to balance these energies within your own being.

The stories of the ancient people often tie their lunar deities to the ocean as well. For the Greeks, their Moon goddess Selene was said to have bathed in the sparkling waters of the ocean when the Moon was particularly bright. In North America, there is the Hawaiian goddess Mo'olelo, the goddess of the moon and the ocean.

The water element, tied to the Moon and the Divine Feminine, can teach us how to get in touch with, or more deeply connect to, our intuition and psychic abilities. The element is also very healing in nature, much like the mother aspect of the triple Moon goddesses, Maiden, Mother, and Crone. We can combine water magick with the corresponding Moon phases to optimize healing and also to influence our dreams, manifestation, and fertility. It will even help us dive into our own dark abyss for shadow work.

SALT WATER VS. FRESH WATER

Is salt water really that much different than freshwater? Yes, both in its chemical makeup and energy. Water found in the ocean is considerably different from that of freshwater lakes and rivers. The

composition found in our seas and oceans
has a salinity, or dissolved salt content
in a body of water, that can vary slightly
from sea to sea and ocean to ocean. It is usually
around 3.5 percent, or 35 grams of salt, for every
1 liter of seawater.[2] However, you can call on the energy of seawater
for the rituals in this book with a glass of fresh water mixed with a
teaspoon of salt.

As you begin to work with salt water, you'll find that there
are definite energetic differences in comparison to fresh water. Lakes
and rivers do not hold the volume that our seas and oceans do, and so
the vibrational energies are different. Rivers are continually flowing,
containing consistently changing energies based on the environment.
A river or large creek often feeds lakes with its vibrational magick.
That lake then goes on to feed another body of water and adds to its
overall energetic makeup. This abundance of energy eventually spills
out into the ocean in an influx of magick. Imagine this happening in
the many locations in the world where a river or lake meets the sea. It
is easy to see then how the energy of the rivers and lakes are feeding
the power of the ocean with their magick.

We see how the rivers and lakes resonate with the energy of
the land around them, as they soak up all that seeps in. However,
while the sea touches the land at its shore, the majority of its water
never touches upon the land at all. Because of its vastness, the
ocean's energetic makeup is all its own.

The oceans and seas also hold the energy of salt. Salt is a
natural protector and cleanser of energy, making it an ingredient
so often used in magickal workings. Those who work closely with
sea magick may find that the body of water becomes extremely
protective of them once a bond has been formed. We thank the

salt for its willingness to protect those who seek it. The next time you need a cleansing ritual, try going into the ocean for a highly beneficial and therapeutic experience.

Salt water also offers more buoyancy than freshwater. Denser than freshwater, salt water exerts more upward force on a submerged object, helping it to float more easily.[3] One way to work with this in a metaphysical sense is to use seawater in uplifting spells. If something has been hidden, ask seawater to help it float to the surface so that it can be seen.

TIDES AND WAVES

Tidal changes happen twice a day, roughly six hours apart. This change affects the water level, creating high tide and low tide. When the tide comes in, the change from low to high tide is often called the "flood tide." The transition from high to low tide is called the "ebb tide."

Ruled by the Moon, her gravitational pull causes these tidal changes, with the water bulging on the side of the Earth closest to and farthest from the Moon. Average tidal ranges are higher during

the full and new Moon.[4] The energy of these moons is more intense, so for those who feel the pull of the ocean as well, time spent near it during these phases is even more powerful.

On top of the tides, the waves that make it to shore hold a different vibrational energy than those that are found at sea. As these waves come in, they bring the power and energy of the deep blue with it. Waves also have the power to take things with them. Ask the sea to help you carry away things that are no longer serving you, including doubts, worries, or fears.

Charged with Moon vibrations, protective energy, and cleansing properties, walking into the ocean, one can feel how different and magickal it truly is.

POWER OF THE OCEAN

Part of the ocean's power comes from its sheer vastness. Our seas and oceans really are the "last frontier." More than 80 percent of our oceans have never been explored and remain unmapped. At this point, we know more about the Universe and space around us than we do the vast, deep blue waters of Earth. There is power in the unknown, and with so much uncharted territory, it lends itself to great mystery and magick.

Much of the ocean consists of dark depths and there is much power in darkness. We surround ourselves in darkness so that we may rest and dream. We plant seeds in the darkness of the soil so they may grow. We reach out into the darkness of space to align ourselves with the Moon, stars, and planetary energies. The darkness is a powerful place of manifestation.

The average depth of the ocean is about 2.3 miles (3.7 km) deep. While sunlight can reach up to 0.6 miles (1 km) below the

SPELL TO CARRY AWAY DOUBTS, WORRIES, OR FEARS

Use this spell to ask the ocean to carry away doubts, worries, or fears.

YOU WILL NEED

- 2 to 3 feet (0.6 to 0.9 m) of sandy beach area
- Something to write in the sand (a stick or ritual knife (athame) will work well)

THE WORKING

1. Approach the sandy beach area with your purpose for being here in mind.
2. Take off your shoes and approach the water, letting it gently lap at your feet and ankles. The salt water will protect you during your working, so you do not need to cast a circle.
3. Move back and stand at the point where the waves will touch your working space.
4. Kneeling down, draw a circle in the sand with your tool. (**Note**: Remember to wipe off or rinse your athame after, if you used one, with regular water because salt water can corrode it.)
5. Write a simple request (two or three words long) inside the circle (i.e., "self-doubt" or "fear of failure").
6. As the waves begin to meet your circle and your words, step into the circle and intone the following:

I call to the power of the sea.
Wash away from me
What is written here,
Whether doubt, worry, or fear,
Of which I have no need.
As these waves recede,
I let the [fear/doubt/worry] go with you.
Cleanse and renew.
Thank you to the power of the sea.
As I will, so mote it be!

7. Remain standing in the circle and feel the fear, doubt, or worry leave you as the waves wash it away.

8. Once it is all gone, take a step back and let the waves wash over the area a few more times before leaving.

TIP ⚜ It is appropriate to leave an offering to the sea for her assistance. This can be the act of picking up any litter you might find in the nearby area. You can also leave a small plant offering that aligns with the water element/Divine Feminine, such as aloe, birch, camellia, camphor, catnip, cherry blossom, daffodil, daisy, etc.

surface, under the right conditions, it rarely surpasses 0.1 to 0.2 miles (0.2 to 0.3 km).[5]

The deepest places on Earth can be found within the ocean. The greatest abyss is found in the Mariana Trench. Its deepest section is called the Challenger Deep, plunging 6.79 miles (11 km). If Mount Everest, the tallest point on Earth, were to be placed in the Challenger Deep, it would still sit about 1.24 miles (2 km) beneath the surface.[6]

There is no sunlight that will ever reach her greatest depths. Neither can humans survive such depths due to the intense pressure of being so far beneath the surface. Knowing the risks, we continue to dive and explore, thirsting for the knowledge and wisdom that the ocean and its depths can offer us. When you choose to explore, you open yourself up to possibilities and opportunities that might not have been possible otherwise.

The extreme pressure of the abyss can teach us about how we react to the pressures in our lives, whether these be the ones that others place on us or ones that we place upon ourselves. The deep shows us that there is a way to handle stress. It can teach us how not to succumb to these pressures so that we may flourish. While there

◎— RITUAL TO TRAVEL INTO THE ABYSS —◎

Perform this ritual to journey into the deep abyss for wisdom and knowledge. This can also be used for deep shadow work.

YOU WILL NEED

- A darkened room to sit or lie down
- A black candle
- Lighter or matches
- A dark-colored blanket or large cloth
- A timer (you can use your phone)
- Journal and pen

THE WORKING

1. Go into your sacred space, ensuring the room is dark with only enough light to see your altar.
2. Place the black candle on your altar.
3. Cast a circle.
4. Light the black candle and intone the following:

> *I wish to travel into the abyss*
> *Please take me there without remiss.*
> *The deepest, darkest place of the sea*
> *To let its knowledge come to me.*

5. Prepare to travel into the abyss. Close your eyes and begin to go into a meditative state where you find yourself in the waters of the ocean. At the deepest, darkest part of the ocean, sit on the seabed, awaiting the wisdom and knowledge that will come to you.
6. Set your timer for 15 minutes and get comfortable.
7. Pull the dark cloth over you so that you are in the darkness.
8. Close your eyes and intone the following:

> *I am ready for my journey*
> *Into the depths of the sea.*
> *Down to the abyss, I go*
> *To find what I need to know.*

9. When the timer goes off, it is time to travel back to the surface. Let yourself rise slowly out of the darkness.

10. Remove the cloth and write down any messages or wisdom you received within the abyss.

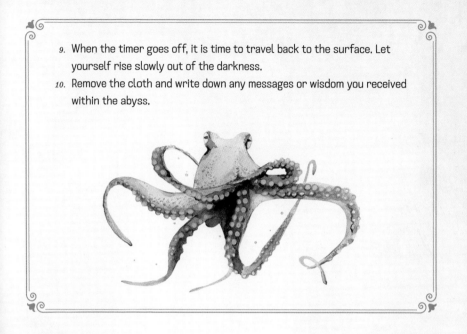

is little to do to avoid a life without pressure, we witches turn to our magickal practice to show us the way forward.

EARTH AND WATER

As we have witnessed, the seas are a place where water and earth come together. Even thousands of feet underneath the surface, the ocean floor holds the power of earth's energy. Through them, we see how two things can merge and yet remain true to themselves. In our lives, we can also come together in profound ways to create something new and different.

The relationship between the elements of water and earth reminds us that there is always a balance to be found. Some aspects of your practice may rely upon something else for it to be used to its full potential. For instance, a lighter brings the candle to life or

❦ SPELL TO SEEK GUIDANCE FOR LIFE'S PRESSURES ❦

Use this spell when you need help from the deep ocean regarding the pressure and stress that life can put upon you.

YOU WILL NEED

- Cauldron or fireproof dish
- A black candle
- A white candle
- Lighter or matches
- Pen and piece of paper

THE WORKING

1. Go into your sacred space.
2. Place the cauldron in the middle of your altar.
3. Place the black candle on the right side of the cauldron and the white one on the left.
4. Cast a circle.
5. Light only the black candle and intone the following:

> *This candle is for the pressures or stress*
> *I am facing in my life at this moment and*
> *also represents the crushing depths of the dark ocean.*

6. Take a moment to write out the stressors or pressures you are feeling in your life.
7. When you are done, light the paper with the lit black candle and intone the following:

> *This pressure, this stress—I give to you,*
> *Into the abyss to see me through.*

8. Very carefully, light the white candle and then the paper, then place the burning paper in your cauldron. Intone the following:

> *The abyss helps me to see the light,*
> *A way to deal with my plight.*

9. You may receive messages on how to handle this stress or life's pressures. Take a moment to write down anything that comes to you.
10. Make sure the paper and both candles burn completely. Make sure all the fire is out.
11. Open the circle.

NOTE ⚡ If you did not get any immediate messages during the working, take note of what comes to you over the next few days. Also, pay attention to your dreams, as messages may come to you there as well.

a cleansing herb bundle to smoke. The ocean shows us how we, too, can bring the elements together so that they may work for us in harmony. There is a balance to all things in life, but it is helpful to know them first individually before combining their powers.

Whatever reason or force has guided you to sea magick, know that while it may seem intense at times, our Ocean Mother is loving, healing, and regenerative. She will welcome you into her embrace like the long-lost child of the sea that you just might be.

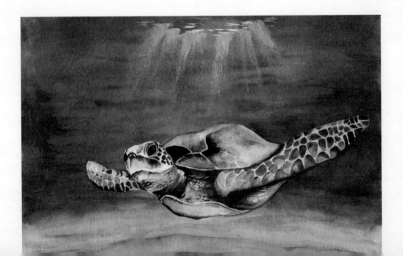

≈ SPELL TO SEEK THE WISDOM OF THE OCEAN ≈

Use this spell when you wish to seek the vast wisdom of the ocean. We will be using a seashell as a buffer to harness the message, as sometimes, what the ocean has to say might be a bit overwhelming.

YOU WILL NEED

- Small dish with water
- A blue candle
- A seashell
- Lighter or matches
- 1 tablespoon sea salt
- Ritual knife (athame)
- Journal and pen

THE WORKING

1. Go into your sacred space.
2. Place the small dish with water in the center of your altar with the candle above it. Place the seashell where it feels right.
3. Cast a circle.
4. Light the candle.
5. Add the sea salt to the water and stir with the athame. If you do not have one, stirring with your finger is fine. (**Note**: Rinse or wipe off your athame after, if you used one, with regular water because salt water can corrode it.)
6. Place the seashell into the now "seawater" dish.
7. With your hands over the dish, intone the following:

> *Wisdom ancient, wisdom vast,*
> *From the ocean into the circle, I have cast*
> *Into this shell, I ask you to imbue*
> *That which I am seeking from you.*
> *Come now, please bring to me*
> *Your message in its entirety.*
> *The knowledge and wisdom of the sea.*
> *As I will, so mote it be.*

8. Continue to let the shell sit in the salt water for a minute or two.

9. Retrieve the shell, and without drying it, hold it to your third eye—the area in the middle of your forehead, just above your eyebrows.

10. Let the ocean's message come to you.

11. Once you have the wisdom she is offering, take a few moments to write it down in your journal.

12. Snuff out the candle. Make sure all the flames are out before leaving the space.

13. Open the circle.

14. Discard the salt water down the drain.

TIP ※ Carry the seashell with you, as it will hold the message and wisdom for a while. Clear its energy when you no longer need it so you can use it again. Also, clear the energy of the candle as it can be used again if there is anything remaining.

THE MYTHOLOGY OF SEA DEITIES

From the depths of the seas come the mighty gods and goddesses that rule the marine life and bring forth the waves and oceanic storms.

It should be understood and respected that not all witches work with deities. For those who do, it is not a relationship of worship but of working alongside them. If you have not worked with a deity in your practice before, you can still call upon the energies a specific sea deity has to aid you.

There is a wide range of sea deities across the globe from virtually every pantheon. The ancient peoples of Earth knew and respected the power of the ocean and the gods and goddesses that were aligned with its energy. Many who choose to work with ocean and sea energy may find that a particular deity has come to offer their assistance, wisdom, and knowledge.

While all of these gods and goddesses hold the power and energy of the oceans and seas, they each have their own unique energy signature and powers, and they are here to help broaden your horizons. Through their mythology and invocations, get to know these gods and goddesses better.

POSEIDON, NEPTUNE, AMPHITRITE, AND TRITON

When we think of deities related to the ocean, one usually stands out. Poseidon, or his Roman counterpart, Neptune. Amphitrite and Triton are also named in this section because of their familial ties to Poseidon.

Poseidon is the Greek god of the sea. He is also the god of water, storms, earthquakes, and horses.

This ancient god is known as a protector of all waters. Seafaring folk relied on him for safe passage, calling upon him for help with navigation on the high seas. As a god of water in general, he ruled over the fresh waters and was viewed as a fertility god.[7] If you need guidance in this realm, call upon Poseidon. He is also known to be moody and temperamental. Those who struggle with their emotions may benefit from calling upon his energy for assistance.

The trident, or three-pronged fishing spear, gives Poseidon the power to set the Earth quaking and crumbling at will. But its main use is to create waves and storms. To the Romans, it symbolizes two things centered around the three prongs. The first is the three properties of liquidity, fecundity, and drinkability. The other is that the prongs represent the three parts of the world: the seas, land, and sky.

The Greek deities had their unique names and aspects, but their Roman counterparts were linked to the planets.

The planet Neptune is the ruler of the water sign Pisces and responsible for our dreams and assisting with psychic abilities. Call upon Poseidon's Roman counterpart to help you with these aspects.

Invocation of Poseidon

Use this invocation to call upon the energy of the sea god, Poseidon. He will show you the power of the ocean and, quite possibly, how to tame the raging storm within when life's emotions threaten to upset your balance.

Poseidon, god of the sea,
I ask that you come to me
With the power of the ocean
Bending to your will, at your call.
Help me to see its might,
To connect with her ebb and flow.
Please show me how
To calm the waters within
When turbulent tides of emotion
Threaten to consume.
The calming waters will resume.

Amphitrite is the Greek goddess of the sea and the wife of Poseidon. She, too, carries a smaller trident of her own. Guardian of the sea and its inhabitants, as a water goddess, she also carries the power of the Moon.

Born a Nereid, or sea nymph, she holds the energy and power of the seas. Amphitrite is considered a sea mother, especially to the animals that dwell there. She communicates freely with sea creatures and is often seen riding upon a dolphin.[7] She and her other Nereid sisters are kind to sailors and help them on their journeys through storms and turbulent waters.

To many, she is not just the goddess of the sea—she is the personification of the Mediterranean Sea. Some assume that she became the guardian of Atlantis after it sank into the ocean, rendering it near impossible for citizens not connected to the fallen city or born with the ocean in their hearts and souls to locate it.

Invocation of Amphitrite

Use this invocation to call upon the energy of the sea goddess, Amphitrite. She will help you become more in sync with lunar energies and teach you how to effectively communicate with the animals of the sea. You will also need her permission and assistance to go to Atlantis.

Oh, goddess of the sea
I ask that you come to me
As the waves break
Under the light of the moon.
Help me to become attuned
And with the creatures
That swim with the ocean-blue
Teach me how to commune.
Amphitrite, goddess of the sea!

Triton is the son of Poseidon and Amphitrite. Depicted as half-human half-fish, he is what we consider to be a merman. Like his father, he has power over the waves. Triton often acted as Poseidon's herald, giving him the title of "messenger of the sea." By blowing into his conch shell, he could tame the waves, either calming or raising them, often creating massive ones if that was his will.[7]

Invocation of Triton

Use this invocation to call upon the energy of Triton to assist you with merfolk communication.

Triton, son of Poseidon
And god of the sea
I ask that you come to me.
What messages do you bring?
From the sea, her vibrant energy,
Or from the merfolk
That live beneath the waves.

PONTUS

Pontus is the primordial sea god. Existing before others, he is the son of Gaia, the Earth Mother, and predates the Greek Olympian gods. As the personification of the seas and oceans, he is irrevocably tied to water, otherwise known as the lifeline of Earth. His power also encompasses those areas where seawater and freshwater meet or are brackish.

While Poseidon is a god of the sea, Pontus is the entire sea itself. Pontus is the father of sea life and the father of Thaumus, the Spirit of the Sea. Pontus holds dominion over the waves and everything that dwells beneath them, including the sea monsters and merfolk. He is the creator of sea life and the seascape—the ocean floor and its abysses, sea caves, and volcanoes. Hydrokinesis, or the absolute divine power over water, is an ability generated from the birth of Pontus. So powerful is he that he can call forth water from nothing.[7]

Invocation of Pontus

Use this invocation to call upon the energy of Pontus to assist you with the extremely vast and ancient knowledge the sea has to offer. Through his world of water, you might also be able to travel back in time, which is beneficial when seeking past lives.

Most ancient god of the sea,
Pontus, I ask that you come to me.
To share the vast wisdom
That, to most, remains hidden.
From the ocean depths
And all her subjects.
Record keeper of time,
Seeing without confines.

CETO

Ceto is the daughter of Gaia and Pontus. A primordial Greek sea goddess, she is the goddess of the dangers of the sea and the Mother of sea monsters and other dangerous marine life such as whales, sharks, and venomous animals. She and her husband, Phorcys, are the parents of the Gorgons, Sirens, and a ferocious dragon called Echidna. She is also well known for her neutrality during the battle between the gods and the Titans.[7] Call upon her when you need a cool and level head to prevail.

Invocation of Ceto

Use this invocation to call upon Ceto when you need to find neutrality in monstrous situations. Seek her help to mediate and see both sides equally.

Ceto, Mother of the monsters of the sea,
I ask that you come to me
When a cool and level head,
To watch what is being said,
And the need to be fair.
Help to mediate with care.

PROTEUS

Proteus is another Greek god of the sea and son of Poseidon, often referred to as The Old Man of the Sea or the shepherd of the seals. He is known for his powers of prophecy—seeing all things past, present, and future.[8] However, he does not easily share what he knows. To obtain his knowledge, one must capture him during his midday slumber and bind him. But beware of his powers of shapeshifting for he will use them to escape. From this power comes the word *protean* derived from his name, meaning changeable in shape or form. If one was able to hold him, only then would he divulge the information they sought. Proteus represents the ever-changing nature of the oceans and seas.

Invocation of Proteus

Use this invocation to call upon the energies of Proteus when you need assistance with divination. Ask him not for the answers but to help you find them through prophetic sight. You will find that Proteus is more willing to guide than to give freely.

Proteus, all-knowing god of the sea,
I ask that you come to me.
Please help me with my second sight,
Knowing divination answers are right.
Guide me to the wisdom
Helping to see what is hidden.

NJORD

Njord is the Norse god of the sea—of its riches and the wind. Njord is the father of Freya and Freyr. As the patron deity of sailors and fishermen, he is invoked by seafarers as well as hunters among the seas. Before setting sail, he was called upon to bless ships. Because of the nature of Viking funerals—sending the departed out to sea on a boat that was then set ablaze—Njord is sometimes aligned with funerary rites. He is also known as a survivor of Ragnarok, the Norse apocalypse. Because the sea was a source of livelihood for the ancient Norse people, Njord is also associated with wealth and prosperity.[9]

Invocation of Njord

Use this invocation to call upon the energies of Njord for spells and rituals for abundance and prosperity. He may also assist you with the strength and courage to survive difficult times.

Viking god of the sea
I ask that you come to me.
The ocean and all its wealth
Helping those sail with stealth,
Surviving with every breath,
Blessing for life and death.

VARUNA

Varuna is the Hindu god of the ocean and guardian of the western direction. One of the oldest deities in Hinduism, known as the King of the Waters, reigns over other bodies of water including rivers. He also influences the time of rain, bringing the seasonal rains, and holds the power over the tides, directing and redirecting rivers.[8]

Invocation of Varuna

Use this invocation to call upon the energy of Varuna when you need help navigating the tides of life or are working with rain magick.

Varuna, Hindu god of the sea,
I ask that you come to me,
Helping to navigate the tides
As the ebb and flow in life.
Give direction and show the way
In the Sun and in the rain.

NULIAJUK (SEDNA)

Nuliajuk is known as Mother or Mistress of the Sea to the Inuit people. She, along with Isarraitaitsoq, is a sea goddess and co-wife to the scorpionfish god, Kanajuk. Together, they live at the bottom of the ocean and rule the depths and sea mammals, such as seals, walruses, and sea lions. When hunts are not proving fruitful for the Netsilik people, it is because Nuliajuk has grown irritated by the sea mammals entangling in her hair often. The animals annoy and itch, and as the goddess becomes more irritated to dislodge them,

she shakes her arms and head, stirring up the waves and making it dangerous for the people to hunt the open waters. The only way to help the sea mammals escape her hair so that the people may hunt again is for a shaman to take a metaphysical journey to the bottom of the ocean.[10]

Invocation of Nuliajuk

Use this invocation to call upon the energies of Nuliajuk when the entanglements of life are proving difficult to unravel.

Sedna, Mistress of the sea,
I ask that you come to me.
Life has grown too tangled
And it's hard to find the way.
Help me to unravel
The problem that is before me.

Remember that calling upon the powers of the deities is not something to take lightly. While they can and will guide you in various aspects of life, their magick can be as wild as the sea itself. When working with any deity, always be respectful. Be mindful of how you call upon them. Offerings made to deities after working with them are encouraged as a sign of appreciation. This could be as simple as cleaning up litter on a beach area near you or bestowing a blessing for our Ocean Mother onto a shell and sending it off in the water.

THE STORIES
OF THE DEEP

The mysterious depths of the ocean inspire some of the most thrilling stories and folklore as well as seafaring cautions and superstitions, for out there, the rules of the land no longer apply.

The stories, myths, and legends told of the oceans and seas are vast, and those that rise up out of the depths are even more intriguing. While some may believe that these stories are conjured from the imaginations of our ancestors, as you begin to work with the power and magick of the ocean, you may find that a lot of these stories have a truth that resonates with you.

We can easily romanticize the ocean when standing safely on land. With our feet planted firmly in the sugary, white sands, we look out to the tropical turquoise waters with a feeling of relaxation, peace, and tranquility. We snorkel and scuba dive to become part of this mesmerizing world for just a brief moment. We "oo" and "ah" at the orcas and whales from the safety of the upper deck of our cruise ships. But what about the more mysterious and dangerous aspects of our seas? What might we learn from their stories?

Plato was the first to recount the story of the utopian city around 360 BCE. He heard the tale from his grandfather, who heard it from the Athenian statesman Solon, who learned of it from an Egyptian priest.

The creators of Atlantis were believed to be half-god, half-human, or demigods. It is believed to have been located in the Atlantic Ocean, west of the modern-day Strait of Gibraltar.

Technologically and spiritually advanced, they had a powerful navy and an advanced society. Its people were connected to the natural world, the Universe, their higher selves, and their deities, and they harnessed and used crystal energy for transportation, communication, and healing purposes.

Atlanteans lived in a true utopia where they had all they needed to be happy and content. However, the Atlanteans soon grew power-hungry and greedy and as punishment from the gods, it was destroyed in its entirety, overtaken by the ocean with violent earthquakes, volcanic eruptions, and giant waves. Atlantis sank to the bottom of the sea, buried so that it would never be found again.[11]

ᛗORE THAN JUST A MYTH

Opinions soon formed that the tale of Atlantis was more fact than fiction. In 1966, oceanographic engineer James Mavor discovered a Minoan city dating back to 1400 BCE in the Aegean Sea. Evidence showed that the city was lost to the ocean due to a cataclysmic earthquake and volcanic eruption similar to that of the fate of Atlantis. And so, theories arose that the lost city had been found.

Until in 2016, the United Kingdom-based company Merlin Burrows, used satellite imagery to find what they believed to be the true site of Atlantis in Spain's Doñana National Park. The team stated that ruins found here included what may have been the Temple of Poseidon, on top of evidence of a long-ago tsunami.

Others are more interested in the tale itself. Plato says it was the greed of the Atlanteans that caused its demise, but many spiritualists who traveled in the astral plane say it was the fault of the world around them. Atlantis's neighbors were primitive civilizations unable to compete with its technological and spiritual advancements. Before war arose, the gods removed the city, using a great wave as a portal to transport it away and protect both its technology and people.[12]

WERE YOU ATLANTEAN IN A PREVIOUS LIFE?

Today, some believe that the following characteristics may mean a previous life as an Atlantean: being extremely spiritually evolved, obtaining a vast knowledge of and connection to crystals, possessing other advanced metaphysical gifts, or being a gifted healer. Use the following to help you get closer to the truth.

- **You both love and fear the ocean.** You see the ocean as beautiful and have a deep love and appreciation for it, but it terrifies you to the point that you will not enter it. It calls to your soul to be near it, but merely touching a toe into the salty waters may bring on a panic. You may also have a fear of drowning.
- **You have recurring nightmares of cataclysmic events.** You have continuing dreams of tidal waves, tsunamis, or even massive volcanic eruptions—possibly reliving the last moments of the lost city.
- **You have a passion for technology.** You're a tech junkie. However, passion goes both ways. You may feel that too much technology is a bad thing that is causing rifts in society and has the potential to be destructive.
- **You are a born sensitive, psychic, or empath.** The people of Atlantis were attuned to the world, people, and the realms of higher vibrations, and you may reincarnate in other lifetimes extremely sensitive to these things. You can easily pick up on messages from the Universe, guides, angels, deities, and your higher self. You may see auras and feel the emotions of those around you.
- **You are drawn to crystals and/or the healing arts.** You feel and easily connect to crystal, gem, and rock energy and use them in your practice. You may even hear messages that come from them. Being drawn to the healing arts is not uncommon for Atlantean souls. All those drawn to alternate healing methods such as shamanism, Reiki, acupuncture, acupressure therapies, or herbal and plant medicine may find that they had a life in Atlantis.
- **You have an ocean animal guide.** You were extremely fascinated with ocean life as a child and adored whales, dolphins, or even sharks. You may have insisted on having an aquarium just to watch the fish. Later on, the sea creature you loved as a child is actually your animal guide.

Just one of these alone does not necessarily mean you had a past life in Atlantis. However, if several of them are true for you, there is a strong possibility that you were an Atlantean.

If you are still not convinced, perhaps working with someone trained in past life regression will help you find the answers you are seeking. You might also try asking your sea creature animal guide if you have one. Or ask the ocean itself.

Remember, if you were given the words of entrance, you can make this journey to visit Atlantis when you feel called to at anytime. If you did not receive the words of entrance this time, you may continue to try. It may be that you need to forge a deeper bond with the ocean before you are allowed to enter the lost city.

Use the guided meditation on page 47 to assist with journeying to Atlantis. It is best to record this ahead of time to play back or have someone read it to you. Drumming often helps one to be able to journey more easily. You will need a timer to call you back if you are working alone. Set it for 30 minutes.

⬦ THE BERMUDA TRIANGLE ⬦

Often referred to as the Devil's Triangle, the Bermuda Triangle is located from the points of Miami, Florida, and Puerto Rico, roughly 500,000 square miles (1.3 million square km) of the Atlantic Ocean. The area has a mysterious and dangerous past dating back to Christopher Columbus when his compass malfunctioned while traveling through the area.

Compass malfunction, electrical equipment going haywire or failing altogether, strange storms, and rogue waves are common in the sea, but those that occur in the Devil's Triangle also include ships found completely abandoned or disappearing without ever transmitting a distress signal. Airplanes vanish from existence, and rescue missions end up missing themselves. More than fifty ships and twenty airplanes are said to have vanished without any wreckage ever being found.[13]

Use this ritual to ask the ocean for her assistance in finding out if you had a previous life in Atlantis.

NOTE ⚝ This spell will be even more powerful if you are actually on an oceanic beach.

YOU WILL NEED
- 2 seashells
- Journal and pen

IF WORKING FROM HOME, YOU WILL ALSO NEED
- Something to play ocean sounds
- A blue or purple candle
- Chalice or glass with water
- 1 tablespoon sea salt
- Lighter or matches

THE WORKING

1. If working from home, go into your sacred space. Play ocean sounds if using. If working on a beach, sit in a comfortable position where the water will barely reach you.
2. If working from home, place a seashell, candle, chalice, and sea salt on your altar.
3. At home, light the candle, then pour the sea salt into the chalice of water and stir.
4. Take one of the seashells into your right hand (for releasing energies within) and intone the following:

A symbol of the sea
For messages coming to me.
But first, I must release
Any blocking energies.

5. Dip the same seashell into the salt water and place it back in your right hand. Intone the following:

Salt water cleanse and wash away
That which might hinder me today.

6. Without thinking about it, feel the energies/blockages release.
7. Place the seashell into the chalice (or the ocean if you are at the beach) and leave it there.
8. Pick up the second seashell, dip it into the salt water, then wipe the salt water from your chakra (above your head) down the line to your third eye chakra (the middle of your forehead, just above your brows) and hold it there for a count of nine.
9. Dip the seashell back into the salt water, then hold it in your left hand (to receive energy). Intone the following:

Mighty Ocean, I ask of you
To bring to me on your waves of blue
Knowledge lost to me
Of a life lived near the sea.
Grand Isles of Atlantis,
Were you home? I ask you this,
Mighty Ocean, I ask of you
Clear messages coming through.

10. Close your eyes and wait a few minutes for the messages to arrive.
11. When you are ready, open your eyes.
12. Take a moment to write down any messages.
13. Keep the seashell in your hand with you for the next nine days, as information may continue to arrive.
14. Thank the ocean for her assistance. Offerings are appropriate.
15. If you are working at home, make sure your candle is completely out and let the seashell stay in the chalice of salt water for at least a day to continue to cleanse it for future use.

NOTE ⚜ If nothing came to you during this ritual, don't worry. This does not necessarily mean that you were not once an Atlantean. It may take a little longer for messages and information to come through, so keep the second seashell with you for a time.

One such strange disappearance was documented by the US Coast Guard in 1967. A 23-foot (7-m) yacht named *Witchcraft* set sail on December 22, 1967, from Miami, so its two passengers could simply enjoy the city's Christmas lights from the sea. Her captain, Dan Burack, made a distress call to the Coast Guard just 1 mile (1.6 km) offshore, stating he had hit something. Although Mr. Burack claimed no substantial damage, he requested help and to be towed to shore just in case. The Coast Guard arrived nineteen minutes later and found nothing. Officials searched the area as well as hundreds of square miles around it for several days and never found a trace of *Witchcraft* or her passengers.[13]

MYSTERIES OF THE BERMUDA TRIANGLE

The agonic line is the energetic line around the Earth that passes through all points where true north and magnetic north coincide. However, the two are about 1,500 miles (2,414 km) apart. The Bermuda Triangle is one of only two places in the world where a compass points to true north instead of magnetic north. This is called compass variation.

The area is also one of the deepest places on Earth, with some of the most complex topography. What starts out as a gently sloping continental shelf comes to an extreme drop-off, creating some of the deepest trenches found, including the Milwaukee Depth, the deepest point in the Atlantic Ocean.[14]

It also contains the Sargasso Sea, located in the North Atlantic. This sea has no land boundaries. Instead, it is bound by four different currents that form a clockwise-circulating system that is the Sargasso Sea. This area is calm, deep, blue-colored water of exceptional clarity and home to the seaweed of the genus

MEDITATION TO JOURNEY TO ATLANTIS

Close your eyes and take a deep, cleansing breath, counting to five on the inhale and eight on the exhale. Take two more cleansing breaths, and then breathe normally. Feel your body grow heavier and heavier, sinking into the place where you are resting.

Begin walking toward a sound in the distance where you will find yourself in tall grasses, and smell the scent of the ocean. Make your way to a beautiful sandy beach and step into the waves.

When the water reaches your chest, a sea turtle appears and beckons you to follow them under. You have no fear; you can breathe underwater. You journey deeper until the sea turtle stops.

Then a friendly dolphin asks you to follow them to continue your dive. It is dark, but you can see just fine. Your dolphin friend will not let any harm come to you.

There is a pulse of palpable energy, and the dolphin guides you to place your hand upon the vibrating, energetic field. You can feel it like a heartbeat. Close your eyes and ask what lies beyond.

When you open your eyes, the goddess Amphitrite, guardian of the lost civilization of Atlantis, is there. Holding her trident to your heart, she asks if the sea lives within you. If she does not see that it is true, follow the dolphin back to the shallows.

If you say yes and she sees the truth, she will whisper the words of entrance to you. You follow Amphitrite's directions and find yourself in a swirling, watery tunnel. At the end of the tunnel is the most glorious place you have ever seen: Atlantis. Take your time exploring. (Let the timer run for 25 minutes here.)

When it is time to return, bid farewell to your guides. Emerge from the waves and sit upon the sand. When you are ready, open your eyes then write about your experience.

Sargassum. All American and European eels spawn and are born in the Sargasso Sea.

The area is also home to extremely sudden and violent storms, arising from seemingly nowhere and without warning. This stretch of sea is also often responsible for determining the strength of tropical storms and hurricanes.[14]

LEY LINES AND VORTICES

Ley lines are energetic lines that wrap around the Earth and are recognized around the globe by varying names.[15] In China, they're called "dragon lines," the ancient Aboriginal people of Australia call them "dream lines," Peruvians call them nasca lines and other South American shamans refer to them as "spirit lines." They hold powerful energy and have strong electromagnetic fields.[16]

When ley lines intersect, they create a vortex, which, in this sense, is a place of powerful, swirling energies. Sedona, Arizona, is also known for its strong ley line energy and vortices.

Twelve points on the Earth, known as the Vile Vortices, are symmetrical and of equal distance from one another along the Tropic of Cancer, the Tropic of Capricorn, and the North and South Poles. Throughout history, these areas have been known to have strange energies, anomalies, and unexplained phenomena.[17]

One of the twelve is the Bermuda Triangle. A powerful vortex is known to open gateways or portals, which would explain missing airplanes and ships. Some theorize that the Bermuda Triangle was once a portal to an alternate dimension or parallel universe that has become less active over the years. Some even say that it's the final resting place of Atlantis. While the last is an intriguing theory, the geographic descriptions do not match.

— Myths and Legends of the Sea —

Beyond the lost civilization of Atlantis and the mysterious Bermuda Triangle, there is no shortage of myths and legends involving the deep blue sea. Pirates are one of many legends of the seas, some of the most notable include Henry Morgan, Blackbeard, Ann Bonny, and Francis Drake. While criminals, they were true seamen who learned the ways of the ocean and claimed a ship home.

Many strange and inexplicable things occur out at sea that you must know all of the good omens and bad omens to be a sailor. It is what keeps them sane while surrounded by an endless ocean for months at a time. From ancient seafaring folk to modern-day sailors, they have an explanation for almost everything, but the whys and the hows cannot always be so simple.

Ghost Ships

One of the most famous ghost ships is the *Flying Dutchman*. The captain of the ship, Hendrick Van der Decken, either challenged an angel or was cursed by a witch. Whichever way the story starts, in the mid-1600s, while en route from the East Indies to Amsterdam, the captain decided to take a shortcut around the Cape of Good Hope. There, he was caught in a catastrophic storm and lost at sea. After, the most famous sighting of the ship came in 1881 from the future King George V of England, claiming thirteen witnesses saw the *Dutchman* that evening. Sailors fear that seeing this ship is a harbinger of doom.

The *Caleuche* is another ghost ship in the waters around Chile's Chiloé Island. She is described as a ship with blood-red sails and luminescent white sides. Termed a demon ship, when she passes, some hear the cackling of her demon crew and see images of beings hopping about with heads that spin backward. People believe the demon crew captures the souls of those who have drowned in the area and keeps them aboard the ship forever.

The *Princess Augusta* ran aground in 1738 off Rhode Island's Block Island while carrying a load of German Palatines seeking a new life in America. When sighted, the apparition known as the Palatine Light appears, making it one of America's most famous ghost ship legends. This ghost ship is known to show up suddenly, blazing in the darkness, during the time between Christmas and New Year's.

Reports of a three-masted schooner on fire in Canada's Northumberland Strait have been coming in since the late 18th century. The origins of this ghostly apparition are unknown. They say the phantom ship appears for a few minutes or up to an hour, sometimes with the ghost ship's crew seen climbing its masts and hearing the sound of gunfire. The apparition appears so real that rescue parties have been called to the scene, only for it to disappear suddenly.[18]

GHOSTLY DIVERS

Along with phantom ships, ghostly divers have been sighted around the world. These sightings have become so well known that several paranormal investigating dive groups formed, searching everything from shipwreck sites to underwater caves.

Off the coast of Santa Monica, California, there is a ghost diver with a pink scuba tank. Similarly, in the Grenadines, a friendly ghost diver wearing a white shirt waves to groups.

Off the coast of Japan, in the Pacific Ocean, is a stretch of water named the Devil's Sea. Much like the Bermuda Triangle, strange occurrences and disappearances of numerous Japanese fishing vessels are reported here. The fishermen here tell an ancient tale of dragons that lurk beneath the waves. Offerings are given to the sea and the dragons in hopes of keeping them satisfied and to lower the chances of becoming one of their victims.[19]

In the previously mentioned Sargasso Sea, several seacrafts have been found here in perfect condition, but with the crew and passengers missing. According to folklore, this is due to the man-eating seaweed that makes its home here. The large accumulation of *Sargassum* can become extremely dense, dense enough to cause ships to become stuck within its mass. The legends state that once the ship becomes immobile, the seaweed goes after its passengers.[13]

ŠAILOR STORIES AND SUPERSTITIONS

There is no shortage of sailor stories and superstitions, some of which were birthed by the ancient stories themselves. Because the ocean is so unforgiving, it is no wonder that there is a long list of both good and bad luck.

One happier story depicts a mermaid stranded on the shore. Found by a Scottish boat builder, he helped her return to the safety of the sea. For his kindness, the mermaid granted him one wish. He wished for the ability to make boats that would never sink. According to this tale, the boat builder's descendants are still building boats, and their craftsmanship is legendary. The story is said to reinforce the importance of paying tribute to the sea and her creatures.

"Ocean madness" is something that has been documented throughout history. One symptom of this "madness" is the affliction known as "calenture." Sailors looking out into the ocean would see a mirage of land and jump overboard. After such instances occurred, sailors would bring the most unattractive woman on board that he could find to work as a cook or maid. If this extremely unattractive woman began to look good to the sailor, he knew he was suffering from ocean madness, and it was time to find a port.

Regarding superstitions, coins are tossed into the sea, especially in areas of known shipwrecks, as an offering to those who lost their life in the water. Some also believe this will keep them in good favor with King Neptune.

To those who sail, especially the ship's captain, the ship is viewed as a living entity—having its own soul, personality, and characteristics. These vessels were given female names after goddesses or mother figures that might nurture and protect them from the dangers of the ocean as well as guide them to safety.[20]

WHO IS THE SEA HAG?

Sea hags often appear as fragile old women dressed in rags. Her true form, however, is an emaciated humanoid figure draped in seaweed with pitch-black eyes, rotting teeth, and long, sharp claws at the tips of her fingers.

Some claim them to be the spirits of women who have met violent ends in or around the sea or on seaside cliffs. Others say they are wicked Fae who punish sailors or coastal villagers for their transgressions against the ocean. They lure them into making impossible deals, and when the human cannot pay the debt, the sea hag takes their magick to sustain her life. Some legends say that they also lure mermaids into exchanging their immortality to become human, much like the tale of *The Little Mermaid*.[21]

Regardless, the sea hag is not to be taken lightly. While they are generally weaker in magick than their powerful sister crone hags, they have the ability to lay nearly irreversible curses on those who wrong them.

Sea hags are proud of their ghastly appearance and have no problem standing up for what they believe is right. They can teach us to embrace who we are, even our darker nature, to love our whole selves. They show us that it is never okay to allow others to mistreat us and that toxic relationships need to end. Calling upon the sea hag can help you have more self-love and self-confidence. In shadow work, she helps you accept the shadows within and integrate them so that you may live your truth, and not just the parts that society deems worthy.

Know that it is *never* wise to ask a sea hag to help you carry out revenge. It could backfire, and you may very well end up in a deal with her that you didn't see coming.

Invocation of the Sea Hag

Use this invocation to call upon the energies of the sea hag when you need assistance with shadow work, self-love, or self-confidence, or if you need help speaking up for yourself.

Ghastly Hag of the sea
I ask that you come to me
Out of the darkness of your cave,
The place you hide beneath the waves.
Your magick flows this way
And is what I seek this day.
Confident and true,
Qualities to imbue,
Love of self and shadows,
Watch it as it grows.
Right and wrong reveals
But with you, I make no deals.
Honor to you and the sea
As you show your magick to me.

Arguably the most famous cursed voyage is the *Titanic*. A fire broke out during its construction, and it was rumored that the cause of it was a coffin lid of a cursed Egyptian mummy in the coal bunkers. A member of the crew, Ramon Artagaveytia, had previously survived a sinking ship in 1871 and hadn't set foot aboard another for forty-one years. Some believe the sea was collecting her due. Her captain, Edward J. Smith, had already been involved in five major incidents, including the *Olympia*, the *Titanic*'s sister ship. He had apparently confessed to his friends that he felt jinxed. Many mediums and psychics were consulted by passengers prior to the voyage and warned against boarding the ship. The day she pulled out of the harbor, they nearly collided with the SS *New York*. If all that weren't enough, fourteen years earlier, Morgan Robertson published a short story about a fictional boat sinking after striking an iceberg some 400 nautical miles off the coast of Newfoundland, the same area where the *Titanic* would later perish. Robertson named the boat the *Titan*. Like the doomed *Titanic*, Robertson depicted a ship that was not carrying enough lifeboats.[22]

Another cursed ship is the SS *Oregon*. The 283-foot (86.3-m) steamship had multiple mishaps before her ill-fated voyage, the most well-known being in 1889, when it collided with a British ship, *Clan McKenzie*. The bow of the *Oregon* pierced the British ship, slicing two sailors in half and sinking the ship. In September 1901, a storm ripped the rudder and rudder post from the ship. In February 1905, the ship's cargo hold caught fire and to douse the flames, the crew drilled holes in the hull to sink and beach the ship in the shallows. On the night of its last voyage, in 1906, a heavy fog rolled in, putting the ship 3 miles (4.8 km) off course. When the fog cleared, they crashed into land. None of the 110 people aboard were injured, but the ship was a total loss.[23]

Cursed from the day of her maiden voyage in 1876, the *Melanope* set sail from Liverpool on its way to Australia. As they left the port, they found an older woman aboard without a ticket. It took three crewmen to get her onto a tugboat to take her back to shore. She fought them every step of the way, then yelled an ominous curse that would haunt the ship until it was left battered and broken. The ship was de-masted on this voyage in a gale. While the *Melanope* did manage a thirty-year career, it was one of strife, including three serious collisions, several strandings and de-mastings, an attempted suicide from her decks, and a successful suicide of one of her captains. Finally, in December 1906, the ship was found by the steamer *Northland*, de-masted once again and heavily listing to one side. While it appeared that most of her crew was able to disembark via lifeboats, the ship was towed to Astoria to become scrap. Stories say that if any captain or sailor knew that salvaged parts came from the *Melanope*, they would refuse them.[24]

SAILOR SUPERSTITIONS: BAD OMENS

Here are some common superstitions sailors believe are bad omens.

- **No redheads on board.** Redheaded people are often said to have fiery personalities. Some cultures consider them to represent death by fire at sea.
- **No women aboard.** One of the most common superstitions among ancient mariners. For one, women were a temptation to the sailors, distracting them from their duties. But more importantly, they believed that women aboard a ship made the seas angry. There are accounts of women disguising themselves as lads to sneak onto a ship. If found, they were bound and thrown into the sea as a sacrifice to the sea gods.
- **No whistling.** It is believed that whistling is a challenge to the winds. Whistling on board a ship will cause the winds to stir and in turn, churn the waves.
- **No bananas on board.** Coming from tropical islands, bananas could harbor deadly spiders and even snakes.
- **Never change a ship's name.** That is, of course, if you want to stay on good terms with the god of the sea, Poseidon, himself. He keeps a record of every vessel's name that becomes sacred to the boat itself. Changing the name is considered a great disrespect.
- **Never say "goodbye" when setting sail.** If these words are uttered at departure, it will curse the voyage, keeping the vessel from returning to shore.
- **"Red sky in the morning, sailors take warning."** Never set sail on a morning that shows red at dawn. Meteorologically, this has shown that rain and potentially devastating storms await you on the high seas.
- **The ship is cursed if the christening bottle does not break.** As a way of blessing a ship, its voyages, and its crew, a bottle of wine, champagne, or ale is broken against the hull. If the bottle does not break on the first try, the ship and her crew are cursed with bad luck.

SAILOR SUPERSTITIONS: GOOD OMENS

Here are some common superstitions sailors believe are good omens.

- **"Red sky at night, sailors delight."** Red on the night before departure is indicative of stable conditions ahead.
- **Cats are good to have on board.** Rats aboard a ship carry disease, get into the food storage, and chew ropes. Having a cat on the ship would hunt the rats.
- **Tattoos are talismans.** Sailors used the ink to ward off bad luck or instill good luck. Nautical stars or compasses to prevent being lost at sea. Anchors to prevent them from floating away should they be thrown overboard. Lighthouses to bring light, hope, and protection.
- **Earrings for protection.** An ancient maritime belief was that an earring protected the sailor against loss of sight and even rheumatism.
- **Traditional good luck charms are found.** Items such as horseshoes, rabbits' feet, and sharks' teeth were all popular charms sailors would secure to various parts of the ship or carry on their person.
- **Painting a set of eyes on the ship's bow ensured safety.** Since ancient times, painting eyes on the front of the ship could help her see her way through anything. This is thought to have eventually morphed into animal or human-shaped figureheads.

Other superstitions and omens include various types of people that should never set foot on a boat (extremely religious people are often considered "Jonahs" and bring bad luck), which foot you step onto the boat with (your right), which days are no-nos for setting sail, etc.[20,25]

MYTHICAL SEA CREATURES

They rise from the depths, these creatures of legend.
They strike fear into the hearts of sailors and stir our imaginations.
They call to us with their powerful magick.

Mermaids. Sirens. The Kraken. Sea Serpents. Selkies. Some of these deep sea creatures strike fear into the hearts of sailors while others hope for a sighting of the magickal and mystical beings. Much like ghost ships and other strange anomalies on the sea, tales of what many consider to be mythological creatures soar to astounding numbers.

With so much unexplored, how can we be certain of what lies in her depths? Some say seeing is believing, while others say that believing is seeing. Unless you have had a personal encounter with such a creature, naysayers may never have irrefutable evidence. Maybe it is left to those of us—the witches, shamans, light workers, and healers who believe in the power of magick and the unseen world—to find and interact with these creatures and their magick.

MERFOLK

Merfolk are sea-dwelling creatures with the head, arms, and torso of a human and the tail of a fish. Males are referred to as mermen, and females are mermaids. Merfolk make their homes in underwater cities protected by magickal barriers. In some regions, they dwell in underwater cave systems. While they breathe air, they rarely stay above the surface for very long.

Although they are generally peaceful and even helpful in nature, merfolk can and will fight if they need to. They possess great physical strength and varying magickal abilities. Merfolk are also known to carry daggers and tridents, as well as scavenged nets, crossbows, and grappling hooks from shipwrecks.

It is believed that most races of merfolk communicate telepathically with one another. However, some have their own audible language and may even adapt our language through exposure.

MERFOLK SIGHTINGS

Encounters with merfolk go back thousands of years. The folklore surrounding these mysterious beings is believed to have begun in ancient Byzantine and Ottoman Greek stories and is now found across the globe.

Around the second century CE, reports were sent of several mermaid corpses washed ashore on the beaches near Gaul. The governor of the city wrote a letter to Emperor Augustus informing him of these findings.

The feared pirate buccaneer, Blackbeard, listed sightings of merfolk in his log books and journals. He had his crew steer clear of these areas for fear that the waters there would be enchanted.

Japanese soldiers stationed in the Kai Islands of Indonesia during World War II reported many merfolk during their time there. Multiple sightings were documented by these soldiers, all describing the same thing: a creature with light pinkish skin about 5 feet (150 cm) tall with spikes on its spine, shoulders, and neck and the flowing tail of a fish.

In 1967, tourists aboard a ferry off the coast of Mayne Island reported a mermaid sat upon a rock, eating raw fish. She was beautiful with long, flowing, blondish-white hair. Another sighting happened just a week later in this same area.

Two recent sightings came with photographic evidence. In 1998, off the coast of Kauai, a boat of ten people saw a mermaid. A local diver captured an underwater shot of her. Then, in 2009, at Kiryat Haim Beach, Israel, multiple people claimed to have seen a young mermaid playing in the waters for several days in a row. The media got involved, and NBC captured footage of her late one night. The area was soon turned into the Center for Coastal and Ocean Research out of Los Angeles, California.[27]

UP CLOSE AND PERSONAL ENCOUNTERS

In early 2012, a reservoir dam in Zimbabwe needed repairs and a new water pump. Local divers were hired and asked to clear the old pumps and pipes. Soon after they began, the divers refused to continue after being harassed by merfolk and fearing the creatures would become aggressive. The government, not believing their tales, hired an outside crew to finish the work. After a couple of dives, the new crew quit after they, too, were intimidated by merfolk. The dam has never been finished.

Daniel Cupido encountered a mermaid in distress in the small village of Suurbrakk, on the Western Cape of South Africa in 2008.

Daniel was with friends when he found the mermaid thrashing about in the water, seemingly stuck. When they tried to help her, she made a keening, sorrowful sound before swimming away. The people here are familiar with the creatures and call them *Kaaiman*, meaning half-human, half-fish creatures that live in deep pools.

In 1718, Samuel Fallours caught a mermaid and kept her in a vat of water in his home. He claimed he tried to nurse her back to health, but she died of starvation after four days of captivity. He drew a detailed picture of her.[26]

There are multiple accounts of sailors tossed overboard from their ships in violent storms, knowing certain death was near, only to be rescued by merfolk. Survivors of shipwrecks have also reported being personally swum back to shore.

With so many sightings and personal stories documented, it's easy to see why so many people hold fast to their belief in the magickal beings of the sea.

MERFOLK MYTHOLOGY

The origin story of the merfolk is around 1000 BCE in Assyria, which is roughly modern-day Syria and northern Iraq. Atargatis, a beloved fertility goddess, fell in love with a mortal man. He did not survive the divine lovemaking, but the goddess became pregnant with a daughter, Semiramis, who would later become the queen of Assyria. Later, Atargatis, still so distraught over her lost love, drowned herself in a lake. But the gods could not truly let her die, for her beauty, even in death, was so great, so they turned her into the first mermaid. Atargatis is still known and worshiped as the mother of the merfolk.[28]

The ancient Greek sea god, Glaucus, is said to have been the original merman. Born a mortal fisherman from Anthedon in Boeotia, one day, while fishing, he found herbs growing nearby.

When he rubbed them onto the fish it brought it back to life. Glaucus consumed the herbs and was made immortal. However, in his immortality, he soon went mad and threw himself into the sea. Instead of dying, his legs grew into a fish's tail, his skin turned blue, and his hair copper green. Distraught by his new appearance, the Titan, Oceanus, took pity on the new god and gave him guidance. Glaucus learned the art of prophecy and became the first merman.[29]

In ancient Middle Eastern mythology, the merfolk were called *kulullu*. Oannes is one of the *apakallu*, or seven sages, described as fish-men in cuneiform texts.

In Scottish mythology, their freshwater merfolk are called *ceasg*. The Isle of Man refers to them as *ben-varrey*, and in Irish lore, they're called *merrow*.

In Scandinavia, *havfrue* is for mermaid and *havmand* for merman. There is also the tale of the *margygur*, a yellow-haired woman who is a fish from the waist down and who drags careless sailors into the depths of the sea. This name translates roughly to "mer-troll."

Chinese folklore calls the merfolk *hairenyu*, and the Japanese people refer to them as *ningyo*. In the Philippines, they have the name Sirena but are called *siyokoy* in the Tagalog language.

The Persian word for mermaid is *maneli*. In Zimbabwe, they are known as *njuzu*.

Some cultures simply view merfolk as deities. The Afro-Caribbean religions call out to their Mother of the Sea, Yemaya. The Jiaoren in Chinese folklore is a race of merfolk that are sought out for their extreme wisdom. Some European texts cite Melusine as a mermaid partaking in tragic stories of forbidden love and transformation. Merfolk have a prevalent and rich history in our world literature as well as personal encounters that it's hard to discount the widespread belief in them.[30]

⟜ PAST LIVES AS MERFOLK ⟜

Today, merfolk fuel our imaginations through aquarium dive shows, aquatic schools, and merfolk groups. While growth in merfolk culture continues to charge our passion for the mystical beings, some of us may have actually lived a past life as a genuine merperson. Signs and characteristics can lead you to the inner knowledge carried in your soul. Like with Atlantis, you can also work with someone trained in past life regression therapy to find answers.

SIGNS YOU MIGHT HAVE HAD A PAST LIFE AS A MERPERSON

Read the following list of traits that often coincide with those who have had a past life as a merperson.

- **You feel the ocean in your soul.** First and foremost, you are passionate about the ocean and her inhabitants. You have an undying love for the sea and a desire to be close to it, needing to live nearby to keep you from feeling out of sorts. Your connection to the sea is so deep that you feel the salt water running through your veins. It is more than just the ocean to you—it's a place that feels like home and calls to you on a soul level.
- **You have a sea creature animal guide.** You have always felt the presence of a sea animal in your life. They guide and teach you and help you feel close to the ocean when you are away.
- **You have an ocean-based career or have always dreamed of one.** If you're not already an oceanographer, marine biologist, or scuba instructor, you want to be. You would prefer to make your living by having a career that allows you to be on or in the ocean.
- **You are drawn to items from the sea or its imagery.** You collect seashells, sea glass, or driftwood. A painting of the wild ocean feels like coming home. You constantly look for new documentaries about the ocean, sea life, or exploration. "Shark Week" excites you. You need ocean

sounds, such as waves on the shore or the song of whales and dolphins, to feel relaxed and be able to sleep.
- **You need to be in the water.** Not just the ocean, you also live for long bubble baths, days spent on the lake, swimming laps, and aquatics class. Sitting next to any body of water brings you peace.

All of these signs point to the possibility of having a previous life as one of the merfolk. Calling upon them might also help you to answer this question.

Use the following guided meditation for an adventure swimming alongside merpeople. It is best to record it ahead of time to play back for yourself or have someone read it to you. Drumming often helps one to be able to journey more easily. You will need a timer to call you back if you are working alone. Set it for thirty minutes. Remember that if you were granted to swim with the merfolk, you may return whenever you feel called to. If you did not receive permission this time, you may continue to try. It may be that you need to forge a deeper bond with the ocean before you are allowed to do so. Continue working with the energies of the sea.

MERFOLK MAGICK

While both mermen and mermaids possess powerful magick, mermaids seem more willing to work with humans.

Merfolk have the ability to communicate with sea life and can assist you to do the same. If you simply wish to be able to commune with dolphins, whales, sharks, sea lions, or have a sea animal guide that you struggle to receive messages and guidance from, the merfolk are happy to help. By helping people communicate with sea life effectively, we learn greater respect for the ocean, and in turn, we are more apt to help conserve and protect it.

Use this spell to confirm a past life as a merperson.

YOU WILL NEED

- ☙ Something that represents the ocean (i.e., seashell)
- ☙ A blue candle—any shade is fine
- ☙ Lighter or matches
- ☙ Journal and pen

THE WORKING

1. Go into your sacred space.
2. Place the item representing the ocean and the candle on your altar.
3. Cast a circle.
4. Light your candle.
5. Focus on the item representing the ocean and intone the following:

> *Mermaid, Merman.*
> *Please help me if you can.*
> *I seek a life I once lived.*
> *And aid only you can give.*
> *I feel that I was one of you.*
> *Swimming under waves of blue.*
> *I ask you to help me see.*
> *If a mer-soul is part of me.*

6. Close your eyes and let the magick wash over you.
7. Open your eyes when you feel like you have given it enough time or if you receive your answer. Make notes in your journal.
8. Thank the merfolk for their assistance, even if you received no messages this time.
9. Snuff the candle, and make sure all fire is completely out.
10. Open the circle.

NOTE ⁂ Keep track of any signs regarding the answer in the upcoming days or weeks. If you do not receive a message this time, you can come back and do the working for the next two days for a total of three times.

Do you struggle to connect with the water element? There could be an underlying fear or trauma related to water. This can include past life traumas such as drowning. If you want to overcome this fear and bridge the gap towards that connection, mermaids can be wonderful allies when healing traumas surrounding water. They can help you with any lingering fears or other issues that block your connection with water in your current lifetime.

Merfolk embody the wild, untamed, and free-flowing energy of the ocean. They can teach us to lean into the freedom of letting go of the constant need for control. This doesn't mean we begin to shuck our responsibilities, only that it's okay to let loose sometimes.

Invocation for Mermaid Freedom

Use this invocation when you need to live in the moment and let go of the need for control.

On the waves or under the sea,
I want the feel of living free,
So mermaid I call to you
Teach me what to do.
Flowing movement and in the now
The mermaid shows me how.
Letting go just to be
In the moment and carefree.

Mermaid magick is what it means to live with the sea as part of your soul. They refresh and renew our spirit as well as the wild, untamed part of us that needs to thrive. They show us how to be more in tune with our physical bodies as well as the world around

Close your eyes and take a deep, cleansing breath for a count of five on the inhale and eight on the exhale. Take two more cleansing breaths, and then breathe normally.

You find yourself standing on the shore of the ocean. Take a couple of steps out into the salty water. Feel the power of the water against your knees, the ebb and flow of the waves. Hold your arms out at your sides to maintain your balance, with your fingertips grazing the water.

Begin to feel a presence with you and follow it. As you tread water, you hear a giggle behind you, but when you turn, nothing's there. You hear it again. Suddenly, a head breaks through the surface. It is the face of a beautiful young woman. She motions for you to go under.

In your head, she tells you her name, that she is of the merfolk. Intrigued, you ask if you can swim with her. If you are not granted permission, it is time to return to the surface. If she gives you permission, you are in for a grand adventure.

When given permission, the mermaid offers a seashell bestowed with the power of breath. With your mer-friend, enjoy the sights of the coral reefs and marine life. She points out various animals and tells you their names. A pod of dolphins wants to play, and you spend a few minutes enjoying their games. Your mer-friend tells you that there is much more she wishes for you to see and asks if you're ready for more adventure. Take your time to swim with the merfolk. (Let the timer run for 25 minutes here.)

When you return to shore, sit upon the sand and look out into the ocean blue. Take a deep breath and feel yourself coming back into your body. Wiggle your limbs out one by one. When you are ready, open your eyes. Take a moment to let it all sink in and then write about your experience.

us. If you have found a friend in one of the merfolk, they have come into your life to guide you on the ways of the ocean, so pay attention to the powerful magick and messages they are bringing to you.

Appropriate offerings to merfolk include seashells, pearls, stones of aquamarine, larimar, or moonstone, as well as combs, and aquatic plants such as water lilies, lotus flowers, cattails, water lettuce, or duckweed.

⊸◇ OTHER CREATURES OF THE SEA ◇⊷

As you may already be aware, merfolk are not the only magickal creatures that call the oceans home. Like the merfolk, these beings appear in folklore across the globe. Let's explore the other beings of myth and how they can help you in your magickal practice.

THE SIREN

In Greek and Roman mythology, a siren was a beautiful female creature with an alluring voice, but sometimes they're depicted as half-woman, half-bird. The sirens, hanging around the cliff sides or rocky shorelines, would lure a ship's crew with their hypnotic songs, causing them to sail into the rocks and wreck the ship, or sway the sailors to jump overboard to follow the song.[31]

Originally, the sirens were beautiful handmaidens of the goddess Persephone. When they failed to protect her from being abducted by Hades, her mother, Demeter, turned them into half-bird creatures to search for her missing daughter. Unsuccessful, they were forced to live their lives cursed as monsters, left with only their beautiful faces and voices. It is believed that they call seafarers out of loneliness but always unintentionally lead them to their deaths.[32]

⌾— MERMAID SPELL TO COMMUNE WITH SEA LIFE —⌾

Use this spell to seek assistance from a mermaid to communicate with sea animals.

YOU WILL NEED

- A traditional blue-colored candle (needs to be traditional blue to align with the throat chakra for communication)
- A purple candle (to align with third eye chakra for receiving messages and seeing animal guides)
- Chalice with water
- 1 tablespoon sea salt
- Lighter and matches

THE WORKING

1. Go into your sacred space.
2. Place the candles, chalice with water, and sea salt on your altar.
3. Cast a circle.
4. Sprinkle the sea salt into the chalice and stir (using your finger is fine).
5. Dip your finger in the "seawater" and rub it on both candles, save for the wicks.
6. Light both candles and intone the following three times:

> *Mermaid, mermaid, I call to you*
> *From your home in the ocean-blue.*
> *Sea life communication is what I seek*
> *Their languages I wish to speak.*
> *Please guide me in this endeavor*
> *So I may talk with them whenever.*

7. Snuff each candle with the "seawater."
8. Thank the mermaid for her assistance.
9. Open the circle.

One might have negative feelings about sirens, but they have the ability to teach us how to make our voices heard. If you struggle with this either out of shyness, a blocked or sluggish throat chakra, the inability to get your point across or believe what you have to say is not important, or that no one will take your word seriously, the sirens can help you. Our voices are important, and we deserve to be heard.

Invocation of the Siren Song

Use this invocation when you are feeling like your voice is not being heard or that it doesn't matter.

To the siren's song I call,
Let my voice no more be small.
My time to be heard is now,
Let the sirens show me how.
Others hear what I have to say,
Knowing my voice matters every day.
The sirens give confidence to me,
As I will, so mote it be!

NOTE It would be unwise to use this or the magick of the sirens to try to sway others to your way of thinking. This energy is merely to help you raise your voice and know that it matters.

SEA SERPENTS

Technically, sea dragons or sea serpents are commonly referred to as simply sea monsters.

Sea serpents represent ancient magick and wisdom. Like snakes, they hold the energy of transformation and rebirth. Because

Use this ritual to call upon the mermaid to assist with healing issues regarding water-centered traumas.

NOTE ❊ This ritual will take place over a 3-day period. You will also need to have a bathtub available.

YOU WILL NEED

- A blue candle
- A white candle
- Cauldron or fireproof dish
- 3 pieces of paper and a pen
- Scissors
- Lighter or matches
- Epsom salt (for the third day/night)
- Bath sponge (for the third day/night)

THE WORKING

1. Go into your sacred space.
2. Place the candles and cauldron on your altar. Have the paper, pen, and scissors nearby.
3. Cast a circle.
4. Light both candles and intone the following:

Mermaid of the Sea
I ask that you come to me
From the depths of the ocean blue
To assist with healing work I have to do.

5. Once you feel her presence, thank her for coming to your aid.
6. Take one piece of paper and write out what you need to release (i.e., fear of water, past life trauma with water, etc.), then underneath it, write, "I release!" Do the same on the remaining two pieces of paper.
7. Use the scissors to trim each of the papers so that it only encompasses your words.
8. Hold one of the papers and intone the following:

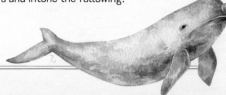

What I now hold here,
This water trauma and fear,
To release so I may heal.
Please, mermaid, help with the ordeal.

9. Using the white candle, carefully light the piece of paper on fire, place it in the cauldron, and let it burn. Make sure the paper burns and the fire is out completely.

10. Sit with this for a few minutes and feel some of that fear and trauma begin to fade away.

11. Thank the mermaid for coming to assist and bid her farewell.

12. Snuff the candles.

13. Open the circle.

14. Leave everything as is and come back to your altar for the next two days to repeat the spell starting from step 3 with the remaining two pieces of paper.

15. On the third day/night, make sure the Epsom salt is available in your bathroom. Start the spell from step 1 and stop at step 3. When you cast the circle this time, make sure it is big enough to contain your bathroom and bathtub.

16. Continue the spell from step 4 and stop at step 13. Sit with this until the paper is ash, and your cauldron is cool enough to handle. Feel the last remaining bits of fear and trauma recede.

17. Bring the candles and cauldron into the bathroom. Draw your bath, sprinkling in the Epsom salt to your liking.

18. Empty the ash from the cauldron into your bathtub.

19. Disrobe and get into the tub, letting the warm water soothe and relax you.

20. Hold the bath sponge and ask the mermaid to bless it with her healing magick. Then gently wash your body with the sponge while intoning the following:

By the fire I was set free,
And now the water heals me.
Let it cleanse and wash away,
For the fear can no longer stay.

With mermaid magick on my side,
To the trauma, I am no longer tied.
By the power of the deep blue sea,
As I will, so mote it be!

21. As you wash, feel any remaining fear or trauma completely dissipate, cleansed away into the water.
22. Stay in the bathtub until the water has cooled. Once you feel refreshed and renewed, get out and watch the water drain the fear and trauma.
23. Once you have dried off, move back to your altar, taking the candles with you. Let them burn out this time if they haven't already.
24. Thank the mermaid for her assistance and bid her farewell. Offerings are appropriate.
25. Open the circle.

NOTE ⚜ If you absolutely do not have any access to a bathtub for this ritual, you can instead smear the ash onto your skin once it has completely cooled and is safe to do so. Then, wash it off in the shower, using the same incantation.

they dwell in the water, they also represent lunar energies and magick as well as psychic abilities.

Chinese culture highly revered dragons and associated sea serpents with royalty and good fortune, while others viewed them as evil foes of the gods and destructive forces against good.

In Norse mythology, the famous sea serpent is called Jörmundgandr, the child of Loki and the giantess Angrboða. The serpent grew so large that he encircled all of Midgard, trapping the people within his coils. He came to represent fate or destiny—that which no man can escape.

Another infamous sea serpent is the multi-headed Hydra in Greek mythology. The Hydra had regenerative powers so that for every head severed, two grew back in its place. Hercules was sent to kill the Hydra as part of his Twelve Labors. He managed to cauterize the necks to keep the heads from regenerating, effectively defeating the beast. Call upon the Hydra to discover your own regenerative abilities.[33]

All dragons are natural protectors and guardians, and the sea serpent is no different. Like other dragons, treat them with the utmost respect. We ask and *never* demand. If sea serpents do not appear when called, they are unwilling to work with you at this time and endeavor to be left alone. Do not take this personally. Sea serpents, like other dragons, do not trust humans easily.

Invocations of the Sea Serpent

Use this invocation to call upon the energies of the sea serpent when you need a guardian or assistance with protection magick.

Serpent of the sea,
Water dragon I call to thee.
With your power, mighty and vast,
I ask for your magick to be cast.
A guardian others will heed,
Your protection is what I need.
Oh, mighty serpent of the sea,
Of this, I ask of thee.

NOTE ⁙ Offerings to the sea serpent are appropriate, whether they come to you or not, as a gesture of respect. Offerings can include fish (left outside), shiny baubles such as coins or jewelry, and things from the sea such as seashells, sea glass, pearls, bits of coral, or sand dollars.

THE KRAKEN

The Kraken has haunted the stories of sailors for centuries. Their tales began in Scandinavian and Norse folklore. An enormous cephalopod with unheard-of strength, and tentacles so large and powerful they could wrap around a ship and crush it or take it beneath the waves.

Historical accounts dating back to the 13th century report massive sea creatures fitting this description. Sailors witnessed giant tentacles appearing from beneath the waves and then slapping down upon the water with such force they were afraid the vibrations alone would break apart their ship. They are also known for their ability to create deadly whirlpools.[33]

Krakens correlate with the mystery and magick of the unknown. They represent what is hidden and, in turn, our subconscious. The magick of the Kraken can show us how to dive deep into our unknown for shadow work, to help us unlock what is hidden or address things that can become all-consuming. The Kraken has eight tentacles, the number of infinity, reminding us that we cannot forever grasp things that we need to let go. When we try to juggle too many things at once, it can lead to ruin.

Invocation of the Kraken

Use this invocation to call upon the energy of the Kraken when shadow work is needed. The Kraken will assist with bringing what is hidden to the surface so you can let go of it if that is best for you and your soul's growth.

Tentacled monster of the deep,
To the surface, Kraken creep.
Show me what I've hidden;
Surface and rise what was forbidden.
Kraken shows the way
Of what will go and what will stay.

SELKIES

The ancient selkies primarily appear in Celtic and Norse mythology. The word *selkie* is derived from the Scottish word for seal. In Scotland, especially the Northern Isles, they are sometimes referred to as "seal folk," who live as seals but shed their skin to come upon the land as humans. Selkies are a powerful symbol of magick and transformation. They also hold the power of duality.

According to the legends, the male selkies were extremely seductive and often targeted women they found to be unhappy in their relationships—particularly those longing for their fishermen husbands.[34]

It is believed that the selkie's ability to shed skin and transform was tied to the tides and the Moon. Selkies teach us that by shedding our true nature, we lock away precious parts of ourselves. If you have hidden away the skin of your true nature, call upon the selkie to show you how to find it and live more authentically.

Selkies show us that being true to who we are is vital for us to thrive. They symbolize the loneliness that can come from disharmony in a relationship. We are reminded that while we may want a partner and a family, the pressures of society and domesticity can lead us away from our true nature if we let it. To avoid feeling resentment or like your life was stolen away from you, call upon the selkie.

Invocation of the Selkie

Use this invocation to call upon the energy of the selkie for transformation and to live authentically.

Seal folk of the sea,
I ask that you come to me.
And show me how to find my skin
So transformation can begin.
With Selkies here to guide,
My true self needs not hide.
I see the magick of these ways,
Living authentically all my days.

Selkies remind us that magick is an important part of life. By living authentically, we can tap into the power of true transformation and transmutation.

Some believe these magickal creatures of the sea still swim alongside the dolphins and fish. Others believe that they now reside in other realms, perhaps Atlantis, having fled the human world when our population grew and began to pollute the oceans. For those who show respect and a desire to work with the sea, the creatures relegated to myth still answer the call of magick and the witch.

THE MAGICK OF SEA ANIMALS

Marine life both fascinates and scares us. They are part of us yet so very alien. Working with the creatures of the sea, learning what it is they have to share, teaches more about ourselves and our magick.

We have no idea how many animals reside in the depths of our oceans. While this may seem daunting or even frightening, for others, it's exciting. The more we explore, the more new species we find. Various marine and scientific publications documented at least ten new animal species found in 2023, including a new whale species in the Gulf of Mexico and the Antarctic strawberry sea feather.

Just like land-dwelling animals, those that make their homes beneath the waves have powerful metaphysical energies and magick. Guides and messengers are not just roles relegated to those on land. Our marine friends, too, have vast wisdom and knowledge to share with us, as well as messages to deliver. Learn how animals come to us as messengers and guides and how to work with the energies of various sea animals and incorporate them into your magickal practice.

WHEN THE ANIMALS COME TO US

Animals come to us for many different reasons, in different forms and different ways, depending on what a person needs. They may come in a corporeal (physical) or spirit form. They may appear in our dreams. Someone new to magick who has not yet opened up to hearing messages from animals will most likely have a messenger or guide show up corporeally. The physical form is more startling, and people tend to heed it instead of dismissing a dream. But this may be more difficult for our marine friends, so do not discount the sudden urge to visit your local aquarium or watch a sea life documentary in your "You might like this" on Netflix. Be aware that if you start to notice recurring images of sea turtles or dolphins, this animal might be making contact with you.

ANIMAL MESSENGER

An animal messenger comes to a person specifically to deliver a message from their higher self, the Universe, Spirit, their guides, ancestors, or a deity. These messengers can come in the corporeal form of a rabbit or deer on a hike or an owl in the tree in your backyard. However, sea animals tend to come to us through imagery in social media feeds, artwork, and on television. Animal messengers can also come in spirit form in a dream or possibly seen through one's third eye. They may be there for a minute or even a few days, depending on how long it takes you to acknowledge the message or if the message is of a more complex nature.

BEING OPEN TO MESSAGES

When animals deliver messages, it can be easy to dismiss them. One must be open. Do not discount the things that are coming through.

If you continue to dream of sharks for an entire week, it is a message. Let them do what it is they came to do.

When starting out, keep a journal of messages, impressions, images, etc. Note the date and time and if there is a later outcome. The more you document, the more you will figure out what is coming through and how it relates to your life. For some, this is confirmation that what is happening isn't something just in their heads.

Messages can sometimes be warnings or something that needs to be addressed. They can also help with spells or ritual timing. They can be from an ancestor or another guide that you have not yet made contact with or from a departed loved one. Animals may also deliver messages through other entities, such as the Fae and elementals.

ANIMAL GUIDE

An animal guide comes into one's life as a teacher to offer guidance, support, protection, power, and wisdom, and to deliver messages. They have a personal relationship with the individual.

Like messengers, animal guides can take a corporeal form or reside only in the astral or spirit realm. They stay for long periods, sometimes for one's entire life. In some cultures, they are often referred to as spirit animals or totems, but we will simply call them animal guides out of respect for other cultures and to avoid cultural appropriation.

An animal guide is often an animal that you feel deeply connected to. Do you often dream of a particular animal? Do you long to swim with the dolphins, or does shark week excite you? If you notice these things about a particular sea animal, chances are they are your animal guide.

Another way to confirm if a particular animal is your guide is to keep track of how and when they show up in your life. If an image of an orca pops into your head every time you are preparing to do spell work or a ritual, then they are likely your animal guide.

⤙◇ SEA MAMMALS ◇⤚

Our fellow mammals that dwell in the sea have to adapt to life in the water. Like all other mammals, they have lungs and require oxygen to breathe. While some may be able to hold their breath for an impressive amount of time, it is imperative to their survival that they be able to breach the water's surface.

With a couple of exceptions, all mammals give birth to live young. Some of them, like seals, sea lions, and walruses, give birth on land. Freshwater otters also give birth on land in dens, but most sea otters give birth in the water. The others that cannot haul themselves from the sea (such as whales, dolphins, orcas, and manatees) give birth in the water, and once the babe is born, the mother assists them to the surface to take their first breath.

Let's look at some of the various mammals that make their home in our oceans and how their magick can help us in witchcraft practice.

WHALES

Whales roam all the oceans and are one of the most ancient creatures still with us today. Because of this, they are considered record keepers of time and history, with their ancient knowledge passed down through generations.

The blue whale is the largest living animal on Earth. They are also the deepest diving mammal in the seas, with the Cuvier's beaked whale diving at the maximum depth of 9,816 feet (2,992 m). Because of their ability to do such deep dives, they can assist us with finding our inner truths and peace for an emotional rebirth.

Whales often live in groups called pods, with research showing strong familial ties. They are known to communicate with one another through captivating sounds we call whale song. Researchers have logged thirteen distinct blue whale songs to communicate finding food, hunting, migrating, and courtship.[35] Calling upon the song of the whale can help you open your throat chakra to assist you to communicate effectively.

Invocation of the Whale

Use this invocation to call upon the energy of the whale.

Diving into the depths
For inner truths and peace,
Surfacing in emotional rebirth,
Changing tides of time.
Whale, keeper of history and wisdom.
He sings his song
To bridge this realm and the Beyond.
Listen and you shall know.

NARWHALS

Narwhals are technically a type of whale that also live in peaceful groups of approximately eight to twelve. A longhorn, or tusk, sets them apart. The tusk ranges in length from 12 to 18 feet (3.7 to 5.5 m) and earns them the nickname of "unicorns of the sea." Researchers are unsure of the purpose of the tusk since there is no documentation of it being used in fights. A common theory is that it is used to gather information around them, which translates to the magickal gift of clairsentience.[35]

As with unicorns, the horn of a narwhal symbolizes a connection to the Universe. The narwhal may show up with messages regarding your magickal practice—they show you how to first look within to find your magick and then send it out into the world.

Invocation of the Narwhal

Use this invocation to call upon the energy of the narwhal.

Unicorn of the sea
Open the magick within me.
Connecting to the Universe,
With horn and wand alike,
The narwhal shows
How the power flows.

ᴅOLPHINS

Dolphins are beloved creatures with a fun and playful nature, intelligence, curiosity, adorable chatter, and seemingly ever-present smile. Thirty-six dolphin species are found in every ocean, with a few found in freshwater rivers.

Famous for their use of echolocation to hunt, and to find their way in the dark, calling upon the energy of a dolphin can assist you with finding your way when you feel lost in the dark.

Extremely social animals, they communicate with clicks, squeaks, and whistles with different dialects in different regions. Like the whale, calling on the dolphin can help you when communication issues arise. They can also help you to be more outgoing, if this is something you wish to change.

Dolphins are believed to engage in play for fun. Call on dolphin energy if you find yourself needing help with the work/play balance in your life. Wild dolphins have also approached humans in the sea to aid them when they are in distress. Call upon the dolphin in times of distress or when you need a fierce protector.

Believed to be one of the most intelligent animals on Earth, dolphins rank up there with elephants and great apes.[35] The magick of the dolphin can assist you when you need to study and retain knowledge.

Invocation of the Dolphin

Use this invocation to call upon the energy of the dolphin.

Riding the waves
Playful and joyous
With harmony and balance.
Between instinct and wit,
Speaking from the heart,
And listening too.
A friend to all,
Protector of those in need,
Dolphin swims the seas.

ORCAS

Orcas can be found in all the oceans, but they are more abundant in the colder waters of the northern regions and the frigid waters to the south around Antarctica. Although they are known as killer whales, orcas are actually the largest species of dolphins.

Extremely intelligent beings known for coordinating and carrying out efficient hunting tactics, they communicate through clicks and squeaks and have varying dialects based on region.

Orcas have matriarchal pods with strong and protective leaders that lend warrior goddess energy.[35] Call on the orca if you need to find your own inner warrior goddess. If you suffer from a mother wound or need assistance with healing the matrilineal line, the orca can help you with this.

A symbol of the Divine Feminine, orcas hold the triple goddess energy of Maiden, Mother, and Crone. Female orcas also go through menopause, which is almost unheard of in the animal kingdom aside from humans. Call upon the orca if you are having hormonal issues or need guidance through your own reproductive phase.

Invocation of the Orca

Use this invocation to call upon the power of the orca.

Warrior goddess of the sea
Commanding and protective.
With knowledge of those who came before,
Trusting the ancestors' way,
Divine Feminine energy,
Maiden, Mother, Crone,
Nurtures and guides,
As orca leads her pod.

SEA LIONS, SEALS, AND WALRUSES

Seals, sea lions, and walruses belong to a group of mammals called pinnipeds, meaning fin- or flipper-footed. Pinnipeds spend time on land and in the sea. While the ocean holds their source of food, the land offers refuge, safety, and relaxation, as well as a place to mate and give birth to their pups.[35]

Sea lions and seals are often confused with one another. However, there are a few visible characteristics that set them apart. Sea lions have small ear flaps, whereas seals only have a small exterior ear hole. Sea lions also have large, elongated front flippers. Because it takes a lot of coordination to walk the way sea lions do, if you are feeling clumsy, sea lions can assist you with this. Seals, on the other hand, use their bellies to move about on land as they have small, thinly webbed front flippers with clawed toes.[35] Both can teach us about balance and harmony and how to harness the energy of water and Earth together.

Sea lions are extremely vocal and boisterous and are known to approach humans in the water to play. If you feel as though you'd like to be more outgoing, call upon the sea lion. Seals, on the other hand, tend to be quiet and soft-spoken, and are not a very social species.[35] If you need help learning to be quiet or to be a better listener, the seal will show you how to work with your strengths.

Invocation of the Sea Lion

Use this invocation to call upon the power of the sea lion.

A boisterous bark rings out
From the land into the sea.
Diving sea lion wants to play.
Her personality shining bright
As she swims the day away.
She shows us how to raise our voice
And join with others in merry fun.

Invocation of the Seal

Use this invocation to call upon the power of the seal.

Land and sea
In perfect harmony
Feel the vibrations.
With seal's belly upon the Earth,
Her quiet ways,
Hearing what is all around,
Knowing her strengths,
Swims through life gracefully.

Walruses are slightly different from their cousins because of their tusks. They use them to haul themselves out of the water and onto the sea ice, as well as for protection from predators such as polar bears and to threaten or fight one another, especially males during mating season. Both male and female walruses grow tusks throughout their life.

Walruses also only reside in the frigid, inhospitable climate of the northern tundra. Their thick skin and layers of body fat protect them against these harsh conditions.[35] Walruses teach us about adaptation, how to harness our powers of protection, and how to love the body we have and all that it does for us.

Invocation of the Walrus

Use this invocation to call upon the power of the walrus.

Gentle giant of ice and sea,
Showing us how to love our bodies
And how to adapt and grow.
Finding lessons,
Even in the harshest of times,
Learning our power of protection,
Begins from within.

SEA OTTER

Sea otters are the largest members of the weasel family, consisting of skunks, wolverines, ferrets, badgers, and, of course, weasels.

Often foraging for food alone, they rest together in single-sex groups called rafts. To keep themselves from floating away from their group, they hold hands and even wrap seaweed around one another, forming what looks like a furry raft. Rafting also keeps them from floating out to sea while asleep and allows them to share body heat. If you need assistance coming together in a group, the sea otter might be able to help you.

Otter diets consist of hard-shelled animals such as sea urchins, crabs, and mollusks. They are one of the only mammals that use tools such as rocks to get their food. A loose patch of skin under their armpit area forms a handy pouch in which they store their tools and any foraged food.[35] Sea otters can assist when figuring out a situation and how to use the tools around you to find a solution.

Invocation of the Sea Otter

Use this invocation to call upon the power of the sea otter.

Voice of the inner child,
Life is meant for play,
Joy, and happiness abound.
With loved ones their forte,
Curiosity and adventure
Come what may.
Find the tools you need.
With intellect and wit
Sea otter makes her way.

◦◦◦ SO MANY FISH IN THE SEA ◦◦◦

The saying "there are plenty of fish in the sea" is typically used in romantic contexts, but it is actually based on the vast coverage of the Earth's oceans and the sheer number of her inhabitants. Approximately twenty thousand species of saltwater fish are known, with new ones being discovered every year. Marine crustaceans top that at twenty-five thousand species. There are roughly two thousand species of jellyfish, three hundred species of octopuses, and about one hundred species of marine reptiles. While all of these sea-dwelling animals do not fall into the fish category, the ocean is teeming with the life and magick they bring.

SEA TURTLES

There are seven different species of sea turtles found in our oceans, with the exception of the polar seas. Most of their lives are spent in the water but they also come ashore to bask in the Sun, and more importantly, to lay their eggs.

Sea turtles are migratory animals, known to travel as many as 10,000 miles (16,093 km) a year between feeding grounds and nesting beaches. If you need help traveling long distances, the sea turtle is your ally. The female turtles often return to the same beach they were hatched—their natal beach. Seek them to find your way home.

These ancient creatures pre-date dinosaurs and are relatively unchanged from their ancestors. Sea turtles also have life spans of up to 150 years. Holding the status of elders in the world of animals, they are known to have strong memories and a wealth of knowledge. If you need help trusting or following your instincts, call upon the sea turtle.

Unlike their land-dwelling counterparts, sea turtles cannot withdraw within their shell.[35] They teach us that having a hard exterior cannot always protect us. It's also a lesson that being vulnerable can lead to growth in ways that hiding cannot give us.

Invocation of the Sea Turtle

Use this invocation to call upon the power of the sea turtle.

Sea turtle, ancient and wise,
Powerful instincts will prevail.
Knowledge within your shell.
For growth to happen
You cannot hide.
Endurance to withstand the journey,
And inner compass points to home.

SHARKS

The *Jaws* movie franchise that began in the 1970s changed the public's perception of sharks. Fear of sharks led to widespread panic regarding ocean safety and, in some areas, vendetta killings. From the stigma around sharks, they teach us to face our fears.[36]

The earliest records of sharks date back to 450 million years ago. They can teach you what it means to not only survive but thrive. Let them also assist with time travel spells as well as uncovering ancient knowledge.

Sharks are cartilaginous fish, meaning they do not have a bony skeleton but cartilage, reducing the weight of their skeleton and, in turn, enabling them to conserve energy. Call on sharks to teach you how to conserve energy. Sharks are also polyphyodont animals, which means they have multiple sets of teeth that are continually replaced. Call on them as allies for tooth-related situations.

Sharks have extrasensory perception through small pore openings around their eyes and mouth called ampullae de Lorenzini, which helps them to locate potential prey.[35] Sharks can show you how to work with your extrasensory abilities.

Invocation of the Shark

Use this invocation to call upon the power of the shark.

Grandfather shark
Show me the ancient ways.
Letting the frenzy go,
Face the fears that haunt,
Finding what it means to truly thrive.
Trusting in your instincts,
Sensing what is all around.

RAYS

Rays are also cartilaginous fish. They have flattened bodies, wing-like pectoral fins, and long whip-like tails with barbed, venomous ends. Even though they have a way to protect themselves, they are more likely to swim away if they feel threatened. They teach us to pick our battles, to know when to walk away or when to stay and fight.

Despite their bad publicity after the legendary nature enthusiast Steve Irwin died by a stingray, these animals are actually quite docile and friendly. They even go so far as to ask for back rubs. Call on them when seeking out new friendships or relationships.

Rays have shown intelligence and exhibit complex behaviors, including problem-solving skills and human recognition. Manta rays have even passed the mirror test, showing the ability to self-recognize.[35] If you wish to be more self-aware, call upon the rays.

Rays seem to glide through the water effortlessly, whether in the shallows or in the depths of intense pressures. They show us how we, too, can navigate life and its varying situations and pressures.

Invocation of the Ray

Use this invocation to call upon the power of the ray.

Fly through the water,
Gliding through life with grace.
Bringing self-awareness to the surface,
Have the courage to make your leap,
Knowing you have the strength to soar,
When to leave, and when to fight.
With the ray, I take flight.

OCTOPUSES

The octopus belongs to the family group called cephalopods, meaning "head foot." Arguably one of the most intelligent sea creatures, they have incredible problem-solving abilities. They are known for learning how to escape their enclosures while in captivity, as well as playing tricks on their captors. Find a powerful ally in the octopus when problem-solving.

Their body composition is truly fascinating. Two-thirds of their neurons are located in their arms, meaning, their arms have a mind of their own. Call upon the octopus to show you how to work efficiently and learn to multitask when the need arises.

Their suction cups have a sense of smell and taste that helps them to collect information about the world around them, as well as gives them the ability to hold items. Let the octopus guide you in situations when you should hold on and when you need to let go.

Octopuses also have three hearts, two responsible for moving blood beyond the gills and a third to keep the circulation of oxygen flowing to the organs and muscles. The third stops beating while they swim, during which they grow exhausted and resort to crawling. Call upon the octopus if you feel your heart chakra has become sluggish or blocked.

All octopuses are venomous through their beaks, but, like snakes, octopuses would rather save their venom for food. Instead, they often use their ink to escape, for it burns the eyes and temporarily impairs the sense of smell and taste.[35] The octopus is the perfect ally for defensive magick and protection spells.

Invocation of the Octopus

Use this invocation to call upon the power of the octopus.

When the solution escapes you
Octopus's problem-solving mind
Ponders and shows the way.
Learning when to hold on
And when to let go
Sometimes, we must defend
Others and open our hearts.
Octopus will guide me now.

FISH

Our fishy friends, in general, show us how living in a group or community can be beneficial to us. However, be mindful that it can lead to losing one's identity if one gets too caught up in others. The fish is the symbol of the zodiac water sign, Pisces, and is tied to the subconscious, intuition, the dream world, and the ability to swim in deep emotional waters. With approximately twenty thousand different species of fish in the ocean, they are too numerous to even try to break down into groups. Instead, we'll focus on the anglerfish as they can help with shadow work.

Deep within our souls lies our shadow self. The shadow is the little parts of ourselves that we hide away. Sometimes it is a conscious choice, and sometimes it is not. Anything can be relegated to the shadow, whether inappropriate, bad, or negative attributes. They can stem from familial or societal conditioning, trauma, or even just our own insecurities about who we truly are.

Shadow work means taking a deep dive into the abyss. It means acknowledging our darker parts and coming to terms with them. Before, the belief was that when we found these hidden aspects, we were supposed to bring them into the light so that they were no longer dark. Today, it is more beneficial to acknowledge your darkness, embrace it, and integrate it as part of your whole being. I believe this is where the term "dancing with your demons" was coined.

Shadow work can be done through meditation, shamanic journey work, rituals, and spell work, and is especially powerful when assisted by an animal guide and their power. Animal energy is a wonderful tool for this because they are unapologetically themselves.

While there are various sea animals that can assist with shadow work, for this working, we will call upon the energy of the anglerfish. This fish lives in the depths of the ocean in total darkness. A bony fin protrusion on its head glows with a symbiotic luminescent bacterium at the tip. Its glow attracts other fish or deep sea creatures straight into its mouth.[35] The energy of the anglerfish represents the unseen world or the place your shadow self resides. It shows you how to navigate that darkness and shows that there is always a light that will see you through. It is a reminder that darkness as well as light is part of the whole being, helping you to integrate both aspects into a harmonious balance.

It is always a good idea to let someone know you are diving into shadow work before beginning. Have a family member, trusted friend, or therapist available once you are done. Doing this type of work is meant to bring up things that have been hidden away, which can include trauma or abuse. Shadow work is meant to be a step in healing your overall being.

⌬ RITUAL AND MEDITATION FOR DEEP SHADOW WORK ⌬

Use this working when you are being called or guided to do deep shadow work. Remember that this is best done when the meditation part is recorded ahead of time.

TIP ⚡ Search for a picture of the anglerfish ahead of time so you know what he looks like.

YOU WILL NEED

- A comfortable space where you will not be disturbed
- A black candle (to assist with breaking bad habits and put an end to unhealthy situations)
- A white candle (to promote healing)
- Lighter or matches
- Something to record this guided meditation so you can play it back
- A timer
- Journal and pen
- Dish to pour candle wax into
- A clear glass jar with a lid

THE WORKING

1. Go into your sacred space.
2. Place the black and white candles next to each other on your altar.
3. Cast a circle.
4. Light the white candle first and say, "This is for my light."
5. Light the black candle and say, "This is for my darkness."
6. Intone the following three times:

Within the deep, within the darkness,
Anglerfish, I follow you. Fearless,
I search for what I have hidden away,
Letting your light show me the way
So I may find my shadows.
To lock them away is what I chose
But now it's time to see
The dark that is part of me.

All right here, within my soul,
As I bring together pieces to make it whole.

7. Get comfortable, gather your recording device, and set the timer for 30 minutes. Begin the meditation:

Close your eyes and take a deep breath. Slowly exhale. Take two more breaths like this. Feel yourself relax. Let go of all preconceived notions about what this is supposed to be or what will be revealed. Remember that you are safe, and nothing in these shadows can harm you now.

A long, dark hallway begins to take shape. A small light comes your way. It draws closer until you make out the shape of an anglerfish. While scary looking, you know he is here to help and guide you.

In your mind, he tells you that you are in the halls of your mind and soul. Notice the doors and their labels. Some you recognize, others you do not. They are experiences, memories, some even from past lives. He tells you that you can visit and explore this place at any time, but for now, your destination is somewhere else.

You follow him down the hallway and a spiral staircase. Down, down, down into the black abyss, you follow the anglerfish.

Finally, the staircase ends in another hallway with a single door at the very end with several locks. The anglerfish tells you that only you can open them, for it was you that locked them. They are dials that rotate. Place your hand upon one of them and feel it vibrate. You instinctively know to turn it widdershins. Turn the next one and the next and the next until they are all unlocked. You pull open the door, and the anglerfish swims inside and hovers overhead, his light shining brighter than ever so that you may see what has been hidden in here.

Take your time to see what needs to be seen. Stay here until the timer goes off. Remember, there is nothing to fear. (Let 25 minutes play in silence on the recording.)

When time is up, make your way out, bringing what you have discovered. It is a part of you. The anglerfish tells you that he is happy to help you whenever you need him. You only need to ask. Come back to yourself. Take a deep breath. Wiggle your fingers and your toes. When you are ready, open your eyes.

8. Take a moment to really come back to yourself. Make sure to write down your experience and what you saw, felt, or heard in your shadows.

9. Once you are ready, it is time to begin to integrate that shadow aspect.

10. With a piece of paper and pen, give the shadow aspect or the experience a few keywords and write them down.

11. Fold it and place it in the dish you will use for the candle wax.

12. Pick up both the black and white candles and bring that shadow aspect into your mind.

13. Very carefully, tip both candles at the same time so that their wax covers the paper, allowing it to mix. This facilitates the merging of your light and darkness so that you can live and walk in balance as your whole, beautiful, and marvelous self.

14. Once the paper has a significant amount of wax on it, return the candles to their holders.

15. Place your hands over the dish with the shadow aspect paper and wax and say the following:

My darkness and my light,
Both of these are right,
Never to be hidden again.
This merging, I begin,
All a part of me,
My shadow, I fully accept.

16. Let the candles burn out completely.

17. Use the clear glass jar to store the paper and the candle wax in. Keep it where you can see it. If you do future shadow work this way, put those papers in the jar as well.

18. Thank the anglerfish for his assistance.

19. Open the circle.

CRUSTACEANS

Crustaceans are the shelled animals that scuttle along the ocean floor. The most well-known are shrimp, lobsters, and crabs. All of these animals have hard, protective exoskeletons and pincers. Crabs and lobsters have eyes that sit on top of stalks that allow them to see all around at once. They also gain information about the world around them through tiny hairs on their bodies, which are highly sensitive to temperature, sound, touch, taste, and smell. Crustaceans have been known to communicate by drumming their claws or flapping their pincers.[35]

If there comes a time when you need to create a protective shell, the crustaceans can help you with this. This is not meant to be a long-term thing, only to temporarily get you through a tough time or situation while protecting you from any negativity. **Note:** If you are in an abusive situation, seek help and get out. Spells and rituals are not a replacement for getting yourself to safety.

SEA ANIMALS AND CAMOUFLAGE

Myriad sea creatures rely on hiding in plain sight as a means of protection or to catch unsuspecting prey. Even more impressive than chameleons, octopuses, squids, and cuttlefish have the ability to change not only their coloring but also their pattern and brightness to blend into their surroundings. The leafy sea dragon and stonefish have bodies that mimic their surroundings. Bottom-dwelling fish such as the flounder, the wobbegong shark, and the stargazer fish all rely on camouflage to blend into the ocean floor. Other masters of camouflage include the ghost pipefish, various species of seahorse, the frogfish, and the decorator crab.[37] These animals are powerful allies in cloaking spells and can show you how to hide in plain sight when the need arises.

Use this working when you need time within a protective shell to keep negative energies and toxic environments from getting to you for a short period of time, allowing you to reach a safe space.

YOU WILL NEED

- A black candle (for protection magick)
- Image of a crab or lobster
- A piece of black cloth large enough to cover your body
- Lighter or matches

THE WORKING

1. Go into your sacred space.
2. Place the black candle and the image of a crab or lobster on your altar.
3. Have the cloth within reach.
4. Cast a circle.
5. Light the black candle.
6. Intone the following three times:

   Crustaceans of the sea,
   I call to you in need.
   Your protective shell that keeps you safe,
   I seek its refuge at this time, in this place.

7. Look at the image that you chose and the protective shell of the animal. Know that sometimes we, too, must seek protection under a hard layer. Remember that this does not make us weak but serves as a way to survive and protect all that we are inside. It is not forever, only to get you through.
8. Pick up the black cloth and intone the following:

   By shell of the [crab or lobster],
   This cloth is blessed as protection.
   It serves as a barrier between me and [the situation].
   As I drape myself in its cover,
   I create my defensive layer.

9. Pull the cloth around your back like a cape. Then, kneel down on the floor, curling up and tucking the cloth around you. Stay here until you feel the magick take hold.

10. Once you feel the protective shell settle into place, stand up.

11. Let the candle burn out completely, making sure all fire is out.

12. Thank the crab or lobster for joining you and for their assistance.

13. Open the circle.

NOTE ⚡ You will need to clear the energies of the black cloth before you are able to use it for other purposes.

Invocation to Hide in Plain Sight

Use this invocation to call upon the creatures of the sea that are masters of disguise when you need to hide in plain sight.

Creatures of the sea,
Those masters of disguise,
Hiding in plain sight,
Show me your ways.
My need to remain unseen,
Cloaking my presence here,
See me no more as I disappear.

SEA PLANT MAGICK

*The plants of the ocean teach us that even in our darkness
there is a reason to reach for the light.*

Most of us witches are accustomed to working with various plant energies, often an important part of our magickal practice. We learn their properties and their magick, how to incorporate them into spells and even food. We burn herbs for cleansing and protection. We ingest others for healing. We put them into spell jars for abundance and prosperity.

The plants of the ocean hold their own energetic properties and magick. If you do not live near the sea, you can still reach out and connect with them by calling on their energy. Others might choose to purchase dried plants in order to work with them physically.

⊶◇ SEAWEED ◇⊷

Seaweed is a broad term for the thousands of different species of marine plants and algae. They function as both a food source and habitat for marine life, ranging from microscopic phytoplankton to giant kelp that grows into what we call "kelp forests." Brown algae include kelp and sargassum, green algae include sea lettuce, and red algae include Irish moss.

Seaweed is typically anchored to the sea floor by a root-like system with the sole purpose of anchoring the plant. In other words, these roots are not responsible for attaining nutrients. Seaweed can be found growing densely along rocky shorelines and into shallow waters. They also grow in the marginal zones where water is approximately 165 feet (50 m) deep or less.

Most seaweed is safe for human consumption. Many people are familiar with sushi rolls typically wrapped with the red algae, nori. Wakame is of the brown algae variety used in miso soup. These plants are rich in vitamins and nutrients.[38]

Calling upon seaweed, in general, can assist with abundance and prosperity spells, summons of the sea winds, merfolk magick, and Sun magick.

⊶◇ KELP ◇⊷

As mentioned before, kelp is a brown alga, the largest variety that grows in our oceans. Kelp makes its home in cooler waters. In ideal conditions, kelp can grow up to 18 inches (46 cm) a day. The giant kelp genus *Macrocystis* can reach heights of 215 feet (66 m). Because of its rapid growth, it has also been used in spells for abundance and prosperity to grow wealth quickly.

They tower above the seabed, creating vast and dense underwater forests and a sanctuary for marine life. Kelp forests also go through seasonal changes.[38] If you live in an area that does not experience much in the way of seasons, call upon this kelp to give insight into their varying energies as well as what it feels like to shift from one to the next.

Kelp holds the energy of water and the Moon and, through that, the Divine Feminine. Witches in history referred to it as The Lady's Tree. Use it to call up sea deities, water nymphs, undines (water elementals), and merfolk.

Invocation of Kelp

Use this invocation to call the energies of kelp if you do not have it physically. If you have never been in the presence of kelp or have not worked with its energies before, have an image nearby. This is a generic invocation where you will need to focus on the exact kelp you wish to call upon.

Dense leafy forests,
Kelp reaches toward the surface,
Reaches for the sunlight.
The Lady's Tree,
Sanctuary for life.
Protection and banishing
And adding sweetness to life,
Brown algae shows the way.

⋙ Sargassum ⋘

Sargassum, sometimes referred to as "gulf weed," is a brown alga. Unlike kelp, it floats like small islands in the sea. Berry-like structures are a big portion of its makeup and are filled with oxygen, which gives it its buoyancy. Use sargassum to assist with healing spells centered around the respiratory system.

Sargassum, like many other types of seaweed, is a haven for sea life, offering both food and shelter. They create mats used as homes and nurseries for juvenile fish and even young sea turtles that make it out into the ocean after hatching. Popping up approximately forty million years ago, the habitat is now home to ten endemic animal species that have evolved to live specifically in this habitat. These species have evolved to blend into the sargassum, so you can use it in cloaking spells.[39]

Within the Bermuda Triangle, the sargassum that grows here holds great energy. If done respectfully, it may help boost your magickal abilities. It can also be used to open or close portals, and for storm and Sun magick.

Invocation of Sargassum

Use this invocation to call the energies of sargassum.

Floating atop the sea,
Cloaking those that hide within,
Calling upon the open ocean,
The wind and the waves,
Sargassum mats spread wide
Vital to life and health.

Sea lettuce is a green alga that, while growing, can resemble its namesake. A widespread plant, it is found along the coasts of the world's oceans. Sea lettuce is highly adaptable and lives at all levels of the intertidal zones. Sea lettuce can assist you when you are going through drastic life changes.

Sea lettuce can reproduce through fragmentation of the thallus like you do with pothos ivy. It can also reproduce sexually. Because of this, sea lettuce is a wonderful plant ally for fertility magick, for humans and animals, and the land where new ideas or actions take root. Use it for manifestation magick. A perennial plant, it is also a reminder of life cycles.[38]

Its bright green-to-yellow coloring can evoke joy and happiness and can be used for such spells. "Lettuce" has long been a slang term for money, making sea lettuce a great choice for money spells and abundance and prosperity.

Invocation of Sea Lettuce

Use this invocation to call the energies of sea lettuce.

Lettuce of the sea
With powers of prosperity.
Cycles of life and fertility,
Drastic changes of life,
Growing without strife,
Helping to manifest,
Love and joy not oppressed.

Irish moss is a red alga that grows on rocks along the shoreline in mid to low intertidal zones. This plant often has a frilly appearance that looks somewhat like parsley. It is most commonly referred to as Irish moss or sea moss. Irish moss beds offer refuge and food for small crustaceans, sea snails, and sea worms, as well as the juveniles of other marine life, such as starfish, crabs, and sea urchins.[38]

Irish moss has medicinal properties to treat gastrointestinal issues, sore throats, coughs, and respiratory ailments. The carrageenan derived from Irish moss inhibits several viruses, including the human papillomavirus, and acts as a prophylactic agent against coronaviruses, including COVID-19. Irish moss can be called upon for healing spells or to boost any treatments being administered.

Irish moss has been widely used in skincare products. Not only does it have a soothing quality, but it is said to have anti-aging properties and UV protection. It can be used in lotions, facial creams, serums, and soaps.[40] Having these properties makes it the perfect plant ally for glamor magick.

Invocation of Irish Moss

Use this invocation to call the energies of Irish moss.

Luck of the Irish
Perhaps comes from her seas.
The moss that grows along its shores
Wealth, health, beauty, and magick
Feeding the souls that call
Upon the Irish Moss!

⊸◇ PHYTOPLANKTON ◇⊷

Phytoplankton are microscopic organisms. Like the other seaweeds, plant phytoplankton rely on the Sun for photosynthesis. They reside in the upper parts of the ocean, close to the surface.

These organisms make up the base of several aquatic food webs for a range of sea creatures, including snails, shrimp, and jellyfish.[38] Because the loss of something so small would impact the entire oceanic ecosystem, phytoplankton reminds us that it is often the little things that matter the most. Call upon phytoplankton to help you find the root cause of something. It also produces a tremendous amount of oxygen for our seas and planet. Metaphysically, this can assist with respiratory and circulatory system healing work.

Phytoplankton are bioluminescent, producing light through internal chemical reactions called luciferins. The light is a defensive mechanism used to startle a would-be predator. Call upon its energy for defensive magick and to bring light to the darkness.

Invocation of Phytoplankton

Use this invocation to call the energies of phytoplankton.

That which goes unseen
We find it reaches far.
The power to affect us all
Healing energies pulse
And magick swirls around.
A light in the dark
A million underwater stars
The phytoplankton shine the way.

⤝◇ SEAGRASS ◇⤜

Meadows of seagrass are considered to be one of the most important ecosystems on our planet because they remove massive amounts of carbon dioxide from the atmosphere. It is also an important habitat and food source for marine life.

Seagrass can only survive in the photic zone, where the rays of the Sun can reach them. Sometimes mistaken for seaweed, seagrass is the only true flowering plant that lives completely beneath the surface of the water. Its roots secure it to the ocean floor to get nutrients. It has stems and leaves and the ability to flower as well as produce fruits and seeds. Call upon the energy of seagrass to assist you with the fertility of your home garden.

It is believed that seagrass evolved from terrestrial plants that took root and recolonized in the oceans around seventy to a hundred million years ago.[38] If you need help adapting to a new situation or relocation, working with the energies of seagrass might prove beneficial. Meadows of seagrass also stabilize the coastal seabed and protect coastlines from erosion and storm damage. If you find yourself needing to calm a stormy situation or an inner storm, call for the help of seagrass.

Invocation of Seagrass

Use this invocation to call the energies of seagrass.

Adapt to change,
Take up root and move.
Yet, being about to ground again,
Finding wisdom in the old and the new,
The seagrass shows us how
To calm a storm
From within or without,
And the waves that threaten to drown.

ENHANCING YOUR MAGICKAL PRACTICE

*The magick and wisdom of the deep blue sea is
as endless as her mysteries.*

There is something extremely calming about looking out into the vast spread of ocean as you stand upon its shore. The waves lapping at your bare feet, the smell of the tangy salty air, and the seagulls crying out overhead. That moment feels incredibly invigorating and powerful. While these two energies are seemingly contradictory, if you feel both of them, then perhaps you are a sea witch.

When you become a sea witch, the possibilities for magick are endless. The bond has been formed with the Ocean Mother and her beaches are a new home for you to explore and burrow into. Combining other magickal practices with sea magick is always encouraged, as most witches are called to by multiple aspects of the Universe. With sea magick, let your magickal practice cast its power out to the horizon where endless wisdom awaits.

⊸◇ ARE YOU A SEA WITCH? ◇⊶

The call of the ocean is something you feel in your soul; you have an undeniable ache to be near it. Going to the ocean feels like coming home—soothing but also recharging. We instinctively know that the sea holds so many of the answers we are seeking. Feel the energy of the tides, the waves, and the sea animals and know there's a special power that lies within the abyss. Sea witches seek out these energies and are able to call upon them easily.

The bond you have with the ocean is something that cannot be explained away. This connection extends to the underwater seascapes filled with beauty, mystery, and magick, including everything we know and everything we have not yet discovered. While an enigma, the sea is our Ocean Mother, and we trust her with our entire being. This is what it means to be a sea witch.

WORKING WITH THE POWER OF THE SEA

Calling upon the energies of the ocean is fairly easy if you live nearby. You feel its power from your home, its energy readily available to you, allowing you to work away from prying eyes. If you don't live near the sea, have no fear as this does not mean that you're not a sea witch or that you cannot work with her energy and magick. Instead, a little more work on your part will be required.

All of the workings found in this book do not require you to be near an ocean. Use the invocations to call the power of the ocean to you, as well as meditations and journey work to visit the ocean in spirit. These experiences can be every bit as powerful as standing on the shore with the waves brushing against your feet.

If you have been to an ocean, these invocations and journey sessions will come easier to you than if you have not. Soon, you'll be able to picture the sea and the way it feels, and the energy will come to you without ever having uttered a word. If you have never visited an ocean, have an image of a beach area or underwater scene you find appealing to help.

Invocation of the Sea

Use this general invocation of the sea to call her energy to you anytime you need it. It can also be used as an opening to any sea magick spell or ritual work you might be doing.

Ocean Mother, I call to you,
Your shallows and your depths,
The ebb and flow of tides,
Crashing waves upon the shore.
The open sea so vast,
Currents swirl fast and slow.
Magick and mystery,
I call upon the power of the sea.

⊙═ RITUAL TO GIVE DEDICATION TO THE SEA ═⊙

Use this ritual to give dedication to the sea.

YOU WILL NEED
- A blue candle
- A seashell
- 3 small sea energy crystals (i.e., larimar, aquamarine, saltwater pearl)
- Chalice with water (without symbols of the western direction)
- 1 tablespoon sea salt
- Lighter or matches
- A guide of your chakras
- A small glass vial

THE WORKING
1. Go into your sacred space.
2. Place the candle, seashell, crystals, water chalice, and sea salt on your altar.
3. Cast a circle.
4. Light the blue candle and invoke the Ocean Mother with the Invocation of the Sea (page 121).
5. Pour the sea salt into the water chalice and stir to make salt water.
6. Hold the chalice and ask the Ocean Mother to bless it.
7. Infuse your chakras with the energy of the sea to bring them into alignment. Using your right index finger, dip it in the salt water and wipe it across your crown chakra. Use your guide for help.
8. Dip your finger in the salt water each time as you repeat on your throat, heart, solar, sacral, and root chakras.
9. Hold the three crystals in your left hand and ask the Ocean Mother to bless them.
10. Place one of the crystals on top of your head and hold one in your left hand and one in your right. Hold your arms out straight at your sides so that a triangle is formed between the three crystals.

11. Intone the following:

I am infused with the power of the sea.
With the Ocean Mother's blessing,
I dedicate myself to her and the sea.
These crystals will remain a symbol
Of the vow I make today,
I carry them with me as a reminder
Of the bond that has formed and is now strengthened
Between me and the sea
And my beloved Ocean Mother.

12. You may place the crystals back on the altar for now, but they are meant to be kept with you. You may want to place them in a small glass vial so they don't get separated.
13. Take the seashell, dip it in the salt water, then hold it over your heart.
14. Intone the following:

I am infused with the power of the sea.
With the Ocean Mother's blessing,
I dedicate myself to her and the sea.
This shell will remain a symbol
Of the vow I make today,
I place it on my altar as a reminder
Of the bond that has formed and is now strengthened
Between me and the sea
And my beloved Ocean Mother.

15. Place the seashell on your altar where it will remain.
16. Dip your left fingers, then your right fingers into the salt water. Place your hands over your heart.

17. Intone the following:

By dedicating myself to the sea
My vow is that I work for her and her health
Whether that is at my altar or on the beach
I will use my magick when called
To help the ocean and her creatures.

18. Let the blue candle burn out completely, ensuring all fire is out.
19. Thank the Ocean Mother for joining you and for her blessings.
20. Open the circle.

STRENGTHEN THE BOND

If you know you are a sea witch and you wish to strengthen this bond, journey to the sea in spirit by playing sea sounds. Like any other journey session, you will need to reach a meditative state. Begin by focusing on the sounds—the waves coming ashore, the seagulls—then focus on the smells like the salty air. What do you feel? Describe the warm sand under your feet. If you burrow your toes into it, is it cooler, perhaps a little damp? Feel the water against your bare feet. It's different from that of a lake or what fills the bath at home. Think about why it feels different. By going through this process, you will be able to reach your beach with a spirit journey. Remember to set a timer to call yourself back if you are working alone.

If you want to dedicate yourself to the Ocean Mother, the following ritual is for you. It is a vow and should not be entered into lightly. If you do not live near an ocean, you might find the ritual acts as a tether and will allow you to call upon sea energies more readily. For anyone who wishes to grow and strengthen their connection to the sea, perform the previous ritual.

The element of water is tied to our emotions. Now that we have dedicated ourselves to the ocean, she can help you understand and settle any unsettling emotions. Begin by creating a powerful sea spell jar to assist with emotional wellness. Emotional wellness can mean getting out of toxic relationships or self-sabotaging behavior patterns. This should not take the place of professional or medicinal support. Remember that emotional wellness does not just apply to depression and anxiety but also creates healthy coping mechanisms, as well as setting and maintaining boundaries.

⚬━ SEA SPELL JAR FOR EMOTIONAL WELLNESS ━⚬

Use this to create a sea spell jar for emotional wellness.

YOU WILL NEED

- A blue candle
- An incense stick
- Lighter or matches
- A medium glass vial with a stopper lid
- Sand (collected from the beach or even play sand)
- A pinch of St. John's wort, lavender, mint, or lemon balm (or a mixture)
- A small seashell that will fit inside the vial (find these at craft stores in strands)
- 1 tablespoon sea salt
- Cup or chalice of water
- Eyedropper

THE WORKING

1. Go into your sacred space.
2. Place all the items on your altar.
3. Cast a circle.
4. Light the candle and then light the incense.
5. Place the smoking end of the incense inside the glass vial to cleanse its energy.
6. Wave the incense smoke over and around the other items. Think about the emotional wellness you are pursuing as you begin to put the spell jar together.
7. Take a pinch of sand and place it in the glass vial. Then add the herb(s) and the seashell.
8. Invoke the Ocean Mother.
9. Stir the sea salt into the cup of water and ask the Ocean Mother to bless it.
10. Using the eyedropper, add the salt water to your vial until it's nearly full.
11. Place the stopper into the vial and use the blue candle to carefully drip wax over the stopper to seal it.

12. Once the wax is dry, hold it to your heart and intone the following:

The Ocean Mother is here with me,
So this spell is all it needs to be.
Emotional wellness is what I seek
With these words that I speak.
By the power of the mighty sea,
What I need comes to me.
This little jar I hold right now,
The spell works, and I allow
Emotional wellness to come to me.
As I will, so mote it be.

13. Keep the spell jar with you. Thank the Ocean Mother for her assistance and bid her farewell.
14. Snuff the candle, and make sure all fire is out.
15. Open the circle.

TIP Let the incense continue to burn—unless you plan on leaving, then make sure it is snuffed out.

THE POWER OF SALT WATER

As you learned in the What Is Sea Magick? chapter (page 11), salt water is not only chemically different from freshwater but also energetically. Salt water is extremely healing, therapeutic, cleansing, and protective thanks to the salt.

Magnesium and other trace minerals also assist with sleep. The sound of the waves can also help to balance circadian rhythms.[41] Use salt water in spells to assist with sleep issues such as insomnia. With ties to the Moon, the ocean is a natural ally when it comes to dreamwork.

Use this spell as a general healing spell. If you live near an ocean, actual seawater is preferred, but you can make your own salt water at home.

YOU WILL NEED

- Seawater (or make salt water with 1 tablespoon sea salt and water)
- A jar with a lid to collect seawater
- A white candle
- Lighter or matches
- A white piece of cloth

THE WORKING

1. Go into your sacred space.
2. Place the seawater in a jar. Then place the jar and the candle on your altar.
3. Cast a circle.
4. Light the white candle.
5. Open the jar of seawater and dampen the piece of cloth slightly. Wipe over the area that needs healing (i.e., stomach ache–apply to the abdomen; headache–apply to forehead; etc.). If this is for energetic healing, wipe down your aura, which resides just outside your physical body, and extend an inch or two. You can also wipe down chakra areas to heal them and issues associated with blocked or sluggish chakras.
6. Intone the following as you use the cloth:

By the power of sea
And all its healing energies,
Let what ails be no more.
This is what I've called you for.
No more illness or pain.
Let health and wellness reign.
By the power of the sea,
As I will, so mote it be.

7. Feel the healing take effect, or if you are working for someone, ask them to let you know when they feel its effects. This might feel like a tingle, or the area grows warm. It may work immediately, and the ailment begins to abate. If it does not, dampen the cloth with seawater as necessary and continue to use it in the area until the magick takes hold.

8. Thank the sea for her assistance.

9. Let the white candle burn out completely, making sure all fire is out.

10. Open the circle.

NOTE ⚝ This does not take the place of seeking medical attention should the need arise.

Salt water is known to rejuvenate us. Its magnesium content can assist with nerve and muscle function as well as help regulate blood sugar levels. When we spend time at the beach and in the water, we also absorb other trace minerals through our skin, such as manganese, boron, calcium, potassium, and cobalt. Salt water has been shown to boost our immune system, and a little "vitamin sea" is now part of some doctors' orders.[42] Use salt water in healing or rejuvenation spells and rituals.

Many witches use water or salt to cleanse their tools or themselves when energies may linger that are no longer needed. Or if they just brought something new into their practice and need to remove anything left over from the previous owner. From what we have already learned, the combination of salt and water can provide a deeper cleanse.

The following ritual can be done in the ocean while wearing a swimsuit as it does not require actual bathing, only rinsing your body with seawater. It can also be done at home in the privacy of your bathtub or shower.

⚘ CLEANSING BATH RITUAL WITH SEAWATER ⚘

Use this spell ritual to cleanse away heavy or negative energies from your energetic field.

YOU WILL NEED

- Seawater (or make salt water with 1 tablespoon sea salt and water)
- A jar with a lid if you are working at home
- A white cloth

THE WORKING

1. Travel to the ocean or make your salt water at home if you do not live near the sea.
2. Prepare to enter the ocean, taking your white cloth with you.
3. Venture out until you are at least hip-deep. If you are worried others will see, you can dip down into the water or go out a bit further.
   (**Note:** When working in the sea, please take the necessary precautions to prevent incidents of drowning or drifting too far from shore.)
4. Bring your energetic field into focus. Find the heavy energies that are mucking it up.
5. Begin to wash your body slowly with the white cloth, taking slow, deep breaths as you do this and seeing all the heavy or negative energy dissolve into the ocean and be carried away.
6. Once you are done with the cleansing, slowly submerge yourself under the water or in the bath at home and intone the following in your head:

The cleansing wash now done,
Heavy energy down to none.
Gone and away from me,
Carried out to sea.
Feeling renewed and free,
As I will, so mote it be.

7. Rise out of the water knowing that the ocean has done its job of cleansing away the heavy or negative energy.

Once you have cleansed all that needed to be cleansed, before performing a new working, it is always a good idea to add an extra layer of protection. Protection spells ensure that the energies in the spell are only ones we have invited. With so much energy and magick surrounding us, there is no telling what may interfere.

General protection spells may come in handy more regularly than you think. It is important to have one ready to perform for yourself or someone you love. While there are many protection spells out there, the following spell is one that you may carry with you wherever you go. As a sea witch, this spell will come in handy when performing workings outside of your space.

DIVINATION AND WATER SCRYING

As you have learned, the element of water is tied to our psychic abilities and can assist with divination. Sprinkle sea salt on your tarot or oracle cards to infuse them with sea magick. Keep sea energy crystals near your cards to help. Douse your pendulum in salt water as long as it's a water- and salt-safe crystal or stone.

Water scrying is a popular method of divination among sea witches. If you have never tried water scrying before, all you need is patience. While some may say that you need a bowl of crystal-clear water, I have found that water straight from the ocean works well. You might choose to add sea salt if you would like to mimic ocean water and do not live nearby.

Find a bowl roughly the size of your face and fill it with the water of your choice. Invoke the Ocean Mother or the sea god of prophecy, Proteus, from The Mythology of Sea Deities chapter (page 33). Let the water become calm and still. Gaze into the bowl, let your vision soften, and see what the water has to reveal to you. You may receive images upon the water, or you may simply feel it. Audible messages may also occur.

⚈═ SALTWATER PROTECTION SPELL ═⚈

Use this spell when you need to carry a little extra protection with you.

YOU WILL NEED

- A black candle
- Lighter or matches
- An incense stick
- A small glass vial with a stopper
- A piece of black obsidian that will fit in the vial
- A sea energy crystal that fits in the vial (i.e., larimar, aquamarine, pearl)
- A sea plant (seaweed will work just fine)
- 1 tablespoon sea salt
- Chalice with water
- Eyedropper

THE WORKING

1. Go into your sacred space.
2. Place the items on your altar.
3. Cast a circle.
4. Light the black candle.
5. Invoke the Ocean Mother.
6. Light the incense and use the smoking end to cleanse the glass vial and the other items.
7. Place the obsidian, the sea crystal, and the sea plant inside the glass vial.
8. Stir the sea salt into the chalice of water.
9. Using the eyedropper, fill the vial with salt water until almost full and close it with the stopper.

10. Take the black candle and carefully drizzle wax along the stopper to seal the vial.

11. Once the wax is dry, hold the vial up and intone the following:

> *Ocean Mother, I ask of you,*
> *Your protection to imbue.*
> *You guide my way*
> *In the dark of night.*
> *You give me light,*
> *Wrapped up safe from harm,*
> *In your protective arms.*

12. Keep the vial with you for as long as you need extra protection.

13. Thank the Ocean Mother for her assistance and bid her farewell.

14. Snuff the candle, and make sure all fire is out.

15. Open the circle.

─◇ THE MAGICK OF THE BEACH ◇─

As you learned in the Spell to Carry Away Doubt, Worries, or Fears (page 18), some magick is best worked on the sandy shores of the ocean. Beach magick can be a powerful way to interact with the ocean, especially if you live in an area that experiences colder temperatures during the off-season and prevents you from going into the water. Perform your workings on the beach to let the ocean carry your dreams and desires out into her waters and help you to manifest them. This is a way to set things in motion. It is a way to let things go.

METAPHYSICAL QUALITIES OF BEACH SAND

As you may recall from the What is Sea Magick? chapter (page 11), the beach is where the ocean and the land touch. It is the meeting place of water and earth with the energy of both elements. In this way, beach sand is extremely grounding and calming. It can relieve fear and anxiety, therefore promoting emotional wellness. It is also uplifting, warmed by the heat of the Sun, and infused with his energy and power.

At night, beach sand holds the power of the Moon as it touches upon the waters of the sea. Through the Moon, it harnesses the power of both the Divine Feminine (water, Moon, and earth) and the Divine Masculine (Sun and fire). Use beach sand to help you balance the two within. It can also be used in spells for strength and motivation.

Beach sand is regularly infused with salt water and is extremely protective. Use it in protection spells and rituals. It also contains clear quartz, making it a natural amplifier of spell work. Place your crystals in sand near the ocean to cleanse and charge them.

USING BEACH SAND IN SPELL WORK

The protective yet calming nature of beach sand makes it the perfect ally for your home. Sprinkle the sand along the outside perimeter to keep it safe from the outside, as well as instill calm, tranquil vibes inside.

Make a sandcastle on the beach to manifest your dream home. As you build the sandcastle, keep the home you wish for in mind. Or, if you are particularly crafty with beach sand, model the sandcastle to look like the home. Say a quick manifestation mantra or write a sigil next to your sandcastle that will bring it to fruition. The waves coming ashore will eventually carry your wish out into the sea.

Since the ocean is our primordial birthplace, beach sand can be used in fertility spells. This can be fertility for you, your partner, someone you love, your land or animals. Approach beach sand as the birthplace of ideas or dreams. Use it in manifestation jars to fertilize growth.

Creating sigils, or symbols that mean something to you or the working, on the beach will allow the waves or the tides to carry them out to sea. This can be for manifesting or letting go. Various sigils can be found online to help you get started. The important thing is that it resonates with you.

⤌◇ WORKING WITH FOUND BEACH OBJECTS ◇⤍

If you have been to a beach, you may have searched for seashells. Beach lovers may have an assortment of items they've found buried in the sand or washed ashore by a wave. Remember that an inclination to see the penguins at the zoo might be an animal guide calling to you. If you are being drawn to beach objects, this may be the sea seeking to form a connection.

SEASHELLS

Seashells are probably the most common thing found along the beach. They are a reminder of the cycles of life and hold divine energy. Once used as a protective layer of the animal that once lived within it, use seashells in protection spells.

The Greek goddess Aphrodite and her Roman counterpart Venus were both born from the foam of the sea and carried ashore in a scalloped seashell.[7] This shell became a symbol of her birth and so it is used in fertility magick. Because the two goddesses both represent love, and are tied to passion and sex, seashells can also be used in workings for self-love and to assist with intimacy in your love life.

Many say that when you hold a conch shell to your ear, you can hear the sound of the ocean. Seashells, especially conch shells, can facilitate communication with the ocean and her creatures. Since the sound of the waves is typically very soothing and relaxing, use seashells with relaxation spells and to assist with a good night's sleep.

CORAL

Coral polyps are plant-like structures you may be familiar with. While coral may look like strange flowers along the seascape, it is actually individual animals colonizing together to create reefs. A mat forms over a calcium carbonate skeleton and as they colonize and grow, the reefs become habitats for all types of marine life.[35] The parts we find on the beach are their skeleton. If you find yourself needing to build a stable foundation for your life, coral can assist.

When waves are coming to shore, ridges of coral reefs act as barriers, reducing the energy of the waves by as much as 97 percent. Use found coral in your spell work to help you set and maintain boundaries. It can also be used in protection spells.

In modern medicine, coral has become a foundation for growing new bone in reconstructive surgeries. Use this regenerative energy in spells for renewal or revitalization.

SAND DOLLARS

Sand dollars are the skeletons of burrowing sea urchins. Because they burrow in the sandy ocean floor, they hold both earth and water energies.[35] The two elements on their own have powerful magick of manifestation. Together, they are unmatched. Use sand dollars when manifesting.

The sand dollar got its name because it resembles large coins. It is said to be a currency of the merfolk. In your practice, they make wonderful allies for spells and rituals for abundance and prosperity. Finding one is also considered a good omen. Carry it with you to bring luck.

DRIFTWOOD

Shaped by the ocean and the sand of her beaches, infused with salt water, and bleached by the Sun, driftwood holds powerful magick of all the elements that many sea witches make their wands from it. You might also make your own set of runes from pieces of driftwood by carving or burning the alphabet into them.

HAG STONES

Hag stones, also known as Adder stones or witches' stones, are usually found on beaches with rocky shores. Water wears a natural hole into hag stones. The hole is said to have powerful protection magick, where anything negative stays out and all the good things in life come through. Many witches and spiritual people carry them as good luck charms or talismans.

Holding a hag stone to your third eye can help to open it. To open your crown chakra and connect to the world of the Divine and the Universe, set it atop your head. These stones can also awaken your psychic abilities and help with lucid dreaming and astral travel.

Hag stones are often used when invoking the sea hag as an offering. Merfolk also carry and use hag stones as currency; they will accept it as an offering as well.

SEA GLASS

Sea glass is broken glass that has been smoothed by the water and sand, creating an object that looks like a tumbled and frosted gemstone. It is, first and foremost, a reminder of the enormous amount of trash and waste in our oceans. Sea glass is litter taken into the ocean and given back to us. She gives us back something beautiful, infused with her energy, to show us forgiveness while also asking us to do better. It symbolizes our Ocean Mother's love and patience.

Sea glass has a diamond-in-the-rough energy to it. It shows you that with a little work and patience, we can do wonders when we did not think it possible. When given something that looks broken, we just might be able to take it and create something magickal.

We are shown that sometimes it is beneficial to soften our rough edges. Transformation can be beautiful. We can grow and change to become what we are truly meant to be while staying true to ourselves at our core.

CREATING A SEA MAGICK ALTAR

One way to bring the magick of the ocean to you and also honor her is by creating a sea magick altar. It does not have to be anything big or fancy—simply a place dedicated to the ocean and your practice as a sea witch. Some things you might want to include are:

- Seashells or other found items like sand dollars, coral, or sea glass
- Beach sand or sea salt
- Images of the ocean or beaches
- Statues, figurines, or images of sea deities or merfolk
- A chalice of salt water
- Crystals with sea energy, such as larimar, aquamarine, or saltwater pearls
- Anything else that reminds you of the ocean

Your altar can be the place to practice workings that require the energy of the ocean. For those who do not live near an ocean or have never been to one, creating a sea magick altar may help you establish a connection and bond with her.

OCEAN FORMATIONS AND SEA WEATHER

The seascape is just as varied as that of the land and there is so much we haven't touched upon yet. Try your best not to anger our Ocean Mother, for when she begins to fight back, she is fierce, a force to be reckoned with.

Wonders are built beyond our eyesight just as the water thrives above. Tucked away miles and miles below, the sandy seafloor is made up of topography that is filled with hidden gems waiting to be explored.

While above, greater forces form on the surface. We know from accounts on the nightly news and social media updates how strong and powerful the weather and forces of the ocean can be. From hurricanes to tsunamis, those that live along the coast know that there is some danger in living so close to the water. These forces can wreak havoc and bring devastation but also powerful magick. We can utilize this energy to work for the Earth, the ocean, and ourselves. We can also reach into the chaos to help minimize the destruction. As you go along in your practice with her, continue to show her respect and honor her mighty force.

⊸◇ SEA CAVES ◇⊸

A lot of sea caves can be found in intertidal zones—places often completely submerged. The ones underwater have parts that are devoid of water. These pockets of air have their own formations, such as stalactites, stalagmites, and ecosystems.[43] Like those on land, they hold the energy of the womb. Venturing into one is to go within the belly of the Mother. Working with sea cave energy can assist with healing a mother wound as well as issues or traumas that have been passed down by female ancestors. Sea caves can also assist with fertility. A place of manifestation, life grows out of its darkness.

Use the journey opposite if you feel that you have a mother wound that requires healing. You can also use it to heal your female ancestral lineage. Remember, recording ahead of time and playing the journey back is best if working alone. Set your timer for 25 minutes.

UNDERWATER VOLCANOES

Unlike the volcanoes on land, those that are underwater have the power of earth, water, and fire. Submarine volcanoes are responsible for creating islands around the world, including Hawaii, Indonesia,

Close your eyes and take three deep, relaxing breaths. Feel your body sink into your surroundings. Find yourself on a boat, out to sea. The weather is calm. The Sun is shining. You hear a splash and a giggle. A mermaid is beckoning you into the water. Jump in and follow her beneath the surface where you can breathe and see just fine.

She leads you to the mouth of the sea cave. She hands you a glowing seashell to light the way and give you directions inside where you will be safe to do your work. Venturing into the cave, the shell gives a pulse of energy to tell you which way to go. The water becomes shallower until you touch the ground.

You rise up until your head breaks the surface. Before you is a large, open cavern with a wide, dry, rocky ledge. You climb out of the water and take a seat. It is time for you to do what you came here to work on. Let the Ocean Mother and the sea cave help you. Let them show you the mother wound or the places where your female ancestors' trauma is currently causing you pain or suffering. Let the work begin. (Let the timer run for 20 minutes.)

When the timer goes off, your work here is done. Pick up your shell and step back into the water. Find your way out of the sea cave in a symbolic rebirth. The mermaid takes you back to your boat, where you climb aboard, and as you do, slowly come back to yourself. Wiggle your limbs one by one. When you are ready, open your eyes. Take time to make notes about your experience.

and Iceland. Because of this, they can be called upon for creative energy. Use it for artwork, writing, or even manifestation spells.

Like all volcanoes, when one erupts underwater, it can be quite violent. Tied to the water element, it can teach us to manage our emotions and keep a level head when necessary. On the other hand, it also reminds us that too much pent-up anger or frustration can lead to an eruption that can cause damage or harm. Call on the fire element when you have a need for self-expression; or if you are feeling pressure from others or society to conform.

⟡ TROPICAL STORMS AND HURRICANES ⟡

Tropical storms and hurricanes may hit the coastal areas hard, but they also influence the weather as storms make their way inland. The sea roils, and waves crash. They are a sailor's worst nightmare. These storms can be a source of panic and fear, but like other natural events, there is magick in them.

Water collected during any storm is often called thunder water. Use it in protection spells as well as other defensive magick. It is especially helpful against psychic attacks. With destructive magick, this water can be useful when breaking curses, bad habits, self-sabotage, or even toxic relationships.

Storms, however, can be considered natural disasters, and so as practitioners, we have the ability to help keep people safe. Most often, we witches can try to minimize the destruction to the places these storms make landfall. Sea witches with a connection to the Ocean Mother can attempt to calm the storm so that when it does reach the coastal areas, it is not as strong.

Incantation to Lessen Tropical Storm/Hurricane Damage

Raise your hands to the sky in the direction the storm is approaching and say:

Gathering clouds and wind,
Those that rip and tear.
Storm surge and waves crashing.
This storm, [name the tropical storm or hurricane here]
I ask that you soften your blow.
Settle the raging power you hold within
So that destruction and harm will not come.
There is no need to battle against the Earth.
This storm, [name the storm again]
I ask you to soften your blow.

NOTE Do not put yourself in harm's way to say this incantation. If evacuations or shelter-in-place are in effect, do what has been advised and work this magick from a safe space.

GALES

Gale winds blow across the ocean until they meet land. While sometimes destructive, they are not as strong as those in more powerful storms. These winds range from 31 miles per hour to 63 miles per hour (50 to 101 km/h) and are defined as persistent gusts over a continued period of time.[44]

Gale winds show us that you do not always need to come into a situation full force but instead with consistency and persistence.

With their continued strength, call upon their power to clear away extremely heavy or negative energy, for they know how to get things moving.

WHIRLPOOLS

A whirlpool is an area of rotating water. Whirlpools are formed when opposing currents meet or run into an obstacle. A vortex is one with a downdraft. Vortices are places where energy pushes and pulls. Use them to gather and store magick and power for yourself or to charge magickal objects.

An extremely powerful whirlpool in the oceans and seas is a maelstrom. These strong maelstroms have the power to pull objects into their depths. Work with this energy to manifest or banish. Much like the tiny whirlpool that is formed when your bathtub drains, those that form out at sea in the Northern Hemisphere rotate deosil (clockwise), with those in the Southern Hemisphere rotating widdershins (counterclockwise).[45] Call upon a whirlpool from the North to help bring something to you. Work with one from the south to remove or banish something.

Whirlpools are also gateways and portals. Use them in journey work to visit other realms such as Atlantis or hidden places such as the realm of Faery.

We are but tiny humans, and our Ocean Mother is so grand and vast. When her storms roll in, she reminds us of her power and unpredictability. She is loving and nurturing, but she is also a force to be reckoned with. While she may work alongside us, offering magick and protection, she also has the power to destroy.

Coming Up For Air

The ocean is life and keeping her healthy is vital to our survival. Protecting our oceans is protecting our future.

You answered the call and bought the book. You took to the ships to learn the tales and superstitions of the sailors. You dove beneath the waves in search of Atlantis and swam with the merfolk. You made friends with the sea animals and even the Kraken and other creatures of the deep. You learned how to work with marine plants and use them in your magick. You played on the beach, felt the magick there, and called to the Ocean Mother. Maybe you even have your sea magick altar set up.

The ocean holds so much wisdom and knowledge and when we work with these energies, we gain insight about ourselves. The ocean guides us to the parts of ourselves that we have not seen yet but that have been waiting on the surface. We grow our knowledge and power and learn how to heal aspects of ourselves with sea magick on our side.

Working with the plants and animals of the sea guides us in our witchcraft and along the journey of life. They may even help us uncover other gifts we have, as well as our purpose here.

Learn more about the ways of the sea and grow your bond with the ocean with the merfolk. They show us how we can swim through life and its challenges, meeting them head-on and with grace. They also act as a go-between when it comes to the more daunting creatures, such as the sirens or sea serpents, who have their own place in our magickal world. But have you answered the question yet? *Are you a sea witch?*

The ocean is the source of all life, the primordial garden from which we all grew. We call her Ocean Mother. Do you hear her calling to you? The same salt water that makes up the ocean runs through our veins and infuses us with the magick of the sea. Can you feel it pulsing within you? The ocean is all the elements—the earth of the seabed, the air that whips the waves, the fire of the volcanoes, and, of course, the water. She offers us this power. Can you sense it?

The majesty, magick, and mystery of the ocean await you. Let her show you how beautifully your magick can unfold when you infuse it with the power of the sea.

Giving Back

Because our oceans are so vital to not only the magick of a sea witch but to our life and life on Earth, it is important that we protect her. Our Ocean Mother is crying out for our help. Part of the responsibility of witches is to be good stewards of the Earth, and that includes our oceans. While we can sit at our altars and work magick for the health of the oceans, those of us with the ability to do more should. If you live near a beach, get out there and pick up trash. Volunteer at a marine life rehabilitation facility. If you cannot physically work for the health of the oceans, teach others about it and why it is so important. Donations can be made to organizations for beach and ocean cleanup as well as research. There are numerous reputable ocean conservancy operations you can volunteer with or donate to. Our Ocean Mother gives us so much, so it is time that we give back, too.

Thank You

Thank you to all those that continue to stand by me, loving me unconditionally through this wild ride.

Thank you to the Ocean Mother for your firm but gentle love and guidance, for your healing and calming spirit.

Thank you to Quarto Publishing for the opportunity to write for you and share the wisdom and knowledge I am granted by the goddess, the animals, and our beautiful, natural world.

ABOUT THE AUTHOR

RIEKA MOONSONG is a Wiccan High Priestess who is currently training to become clergy. She is also an Andean tradition-trained, mesa-carrying shaman. It is her journey, soul path, and goddess-given gift to teach, to share wisdom and knowledge with others, and to help facilitate healing and growth for those on their own journey. She resides in Colorado with her feline familiar, Artemis.

Rieka has always felt the call to work with the sea and our Ocean Mother's energies, even as a child. There was a time when she wanted nothing more than to be a marine biologist. She currently has several ocean animal guides and uses her natural ability to connect with them for wisdom and guidance. It is her dream to help others form close bonds with the sea as well as her plants and animals, and to teach them how to call upon these energies when they are needed.

REFERENCES

1. "Oceans, Ocean Landforms Information, Facts, News, Photos -- National Geographic." Science. October 15, 2009. https://www.nationalgeographic.com/science/article/oceans-underwater.

2. Water Science School. "Why Is the Ocean Salty? | U.S. Geological Survey." USGS science for a changing world. May 23, 2019. https://www.usgs.gov/special-topics/water-science-school/science/why-ocean-salty.

3. Klein, Chris. "Why You Float Better in Salt Water than in Fresh Water Waves." Wave Pool Magazine - for Your Curiosity and Stoke. December 23, 2019. https://wavepoolmag.com/the-lowdown-on-buoyancy-in-a-wave-pool/.

4. Powell, Jack. "Four Biggest Differences between the Ocean & Fresh Water." Sciencing. April 25, 2018. https://sciencing.com/four-between-ocean-fresh-water-8519973.html.

5. "How Deep Is the Ocean?: Ocean Exploration Facts: NOAA Office of Ocean Exploration and Research." NOAA. 2010. https://oceanexplorer.noaa.gov/facts/ocean-depth.html.

6. Raunek. "10 Deepest Parts of the Ocean." Marine Insight. June 4, 2023. https://www.marineinsight.com/know-more/10-deepest-parts-of-the-ocean/.

7. "Sea Gods & Goddesses | Theoi Greek Mythology." Theoi.com. 2017. https://www.theoi.com/greek-mythology/sea-gods.html.

8. Smit, Jana Louise. "Water Gods and Sea Gods from around the World | History Cooperative." March 11, 2014. https://historycooperative.org/water-gods-gods-of-the-sea.

9. Apel, Thomas. "Njord." Mythopedia. Dec. 2, 2022. https://mythopedia.com/topics/njord.

10. Stieger, Allison. "Sedna, Inuit Goddess of the Sea and Its Creatures • Mythic Stories." Mythic Stories. March 18, 2015. https://mythicstories. com/sedna-inuit-goddess-of-the-sea-and-its-creatures/.

11. History.com Editors. "Atlantis." HISTORY. A&E Television Networks. History.com. August 21, 2018. https://www.history.com/topics/ folklore/atlantis.

12. Augustyn, Adam. "Atlantis | Description & Legend | Britannica." In Encyclopædia Britannica. March 25, 2024. https://www.britannica.com/ topic/Atlantis-legendary-island.

13. Luebering, J.E. "Bermuda Triangle | Description & Facts." In Encyclopædia Britannica. March 27, 2024. https://www.britannica.com/ place/Bermuda-Triangle.

14. NOAA. "What Is the Bermuda Triangle?" NOAA. January 18, 2024. https://oceanservice.noaa.gov/facts/bermudatri.html.

15. Kershner, Kate. "What Are Ley Lines?" HowStuffWorks. Nov. 30, 2023. https://science.howstuffworks.com/science-vs-myth/unexplained- phenomena/ley-lines.htm.

16. "Ley-Lines." Ancient Wisdom. n.d. http://www.ancient-wisdom.com/ leylines.htm.

17. Raunek. "Deciphering the Mystery of Vile Vortices." Marine Insight. November 30, 2018. https://www.marineinsight.com/maritime-history/ deciphering-the-mystery-of-vile-vortices/.

18. Laliberte, Marissa. "10 Ghost Ship Mysteries That Can't Be Explained." Reader's Digest. Jan. 25, 2024. https://www.rd.com/list/ghost-ships/.

19. Denny, Megan. "Ocean Stories: Mysteries, Legends and Superstitions." Blog.padi.com. October 20, 2016. https://blog.padi.com/ocean-stories- mysteries-legends-superstitions/.

20. McGrory, Ruby. "13 of the Weirdest Nautical Superstitions." Dockwalk. October 28, 2022. https://www.dockwalk.com/news/13-nautical- superstitions

21. "Sea Hag." Forgotten Realms Wiki. n.d. https://forgottenrealms.fandom.com/wiki/Sea_hag.

22. (Adapted by) Sam. "The Curse of the Titanic: The Dark Legend Surrounding the Most Iconic Sunken Ocean Liner in History." MARCA. June 21, 2023. https://www.marca.com/en/lifestyle/world-news/2023/06/21/6492e69aca474133058b45d4.html.

23. Reamer, David | Histories of Alaska. "The SS Oregon: The Cursed Ship That Could Not Survive Alaska." Anchorage Daily News. February 12, 2023. https://www.adn.com/alaska-life/2023/02/12/the-ss-oregon-the-cursed-ship-that-could-not-survive-alaska/.

24. John, Finn J.D. "'Ship of Romance and Death' met a dramatic end," Offbeat Oregon Podcast. June 14, 2014. https://offbeatoregon.com/1506b.cursed-ships-melanope-343.html.

25. "Top 20 Sailing Superstitions." New Zealand Maritime Museum. n.d. https://www.maritimemuseum.co.nz/collections/top-20-sailing-superstitions.

26. Molly. "Mermaid Sightings Map by Location - Where Have They Been Spotted?" Everything Mermaid. July 15, 2019. https://everythingmermaid.com/mermaid-sightings/.

27. Navab, Ameena. "Top 8 Real Mermaid Sightings You Won't Believe | Ocean Info." Oceaninfo.com. July 4, 2021. https://oceaninfo.com/exploration/myths-and-legends/mermaid-sightings/.

28. Ellis, Carmen. "Fairytales, Myths, Legends and Fantasy…the Three Most Famous Mermaids in History." Majestic Whale Encounters. October 9, 2020. https://www.majesticwhaleencounters.com.au/fairytales-myths-legends-and-fantasythe-three-most-famous-mermaids-in-history.

29. "Glaucus | Greek Mythology." Encyclopedia Britannica. n.d. https://www.britannica.com/topic/Glaucus-Greek-mythology.

30. Kingsbury, Margaret. "No Ariels Here: 16 Mermaids from around the World." BOOK RIOT. August 25, 2019. https://bookriot.com/mermaids-from-around-the-world/.

31. Atsma, Aaron. "SIRENS (Seirenes) - Half-Bird Women of Greek Mythology." Theoi.com. 2017. https://www.theoi.com/Pontios/Seirenes.html.

32. Lotzof, Kerry. "Sea Monsters and Their Inspiration: Serpents, Mermaids, the Kraken and More." National History Museum UK. n.d. https://www.nhm.ac.uk/discover/sea-monsters-inspiration-serpents-mermaids-the-kraken.html.

33. "40+ Stupendous Sea Monsters (in Stories You'll Want to Dive Into)." Reedsy Discovery. June 7, 2019. https://reedsy.com/discovery/blog/sea-monsters.

34. "Scottish Folklore and the Selkie | Intrepidus Outdoors - Edinburgh." Intrepidus Outdoors. August 12, 2018. https://intrepidusoutdoors.co.uk/scottish-folklore-the-selkie.

35. "Ocean Animal Encyclopedia." Oceana. n.d. https://oceana.org/marine-life/.

36. Maycock, Sophie A. "45 Years of the 'Jaws Effect.'" SharkSpeak. December 26, 2020. https://www.sophiemaycocksharkspeak.com/post/45-years-of-the-jaws-effect-1.

37. Roberts, Emily Simeral. "Hide-And-Seek: Ocean Animals with Top-Notch Camouflage." Ocean Conservancy. September 27, 2022. https://oceanconservancy.org/blog/2022/09/27/ocean-animals-with-top-notch-camouflage/.

38. "Ocean Plants: Marine Gardens You'll Find Underwater." Scuba.com. June 8. 2023. https://www.scuba.com/blog/marine-gardens-5-types-plants-ocean/.

39. "Sargasso Sea Commission." Sargasso Sea Commission. n.d. http://www.sargassoseacommission.org/.

40. "What Is Irish Moss Seaweed? Ecology and Human History of Chondrus Cris." Maine Coast Sea Vegetables. n.d. https://seaveg.com/pages/what-is-irish-moss.

41. Pelling, Elliot. "The Science behind the Healing Powers of the Salty Sea." Blog.padi.com. May 29, 2023. https://blog.padi.com/health-benefits-salt-water/.

42. Alexander, Kelly. "The Blue Zone: How the Ocean Heals Body, Mind & Soul | Escape Haven." Escape Haven Women's Retreats. April 29, 2019. https://escapehaven.com/2019/04/the-blue-zone-how-the-ocean-heals-body-mind-soul/.

43. "Sea Caves." National Speleological Society. n.d. https://caves.org/sea-caves/.

44. National Hurricane Center and Central Pacific Hurricane Center. "Tropical Cyclone Climatology." NOAA. 2018. https://www.nhc.noaa.gov/climo/.

45. Harvey, Ailsa. "Whirlpools: Facts, Formation and Survival Tips." Livescience.com. May 11, 2022. https://www.livescience.com/whirlpools.

INDEX